me and my sewing adventure

me and my sewing adventure

adventure

an intermediate guide

Kate Haxell

First published in the United States in 2014
by
C&T Publishing, Inc
PO Box 1456,
Lafayette, CA 94549

www.ctpub.com

Photography Dominic Harris
Design Louise Leffler

This book was produced by
Breslich and Foss Ltd
Unit 2a Union Court
20–22 Union Road
London SW4 6JP

Library of Congress Cataloging-in-Publication
data available upon request.

ISBN 978-1-60705-876-2

Printed and bound in China

10 9 8 7 6 5 4 3 2 1

CONTENTS

Introduction

The best way to learn is to build on previous successes, and that is what this book is all about. It's a follow-on from my first sewing book, **Me and My Sewing Machine: a beginner's guide**, and it's full of sewing skills and techniques to take you beyond the basics. You don't need to have read **Me and My...** to use this book, but you do need to be able to sew a bit.

As well as methods for your sewing machine, I've also included in this book hand-sewing techniques that will help you finish off machine-made projects to a professional standard, and allow you to explore and develop for yourself the centuries-old skills of hand needlework. Today's world is too often in too much of a hurry: cut corners, work faster, take the easier option—and we lose sight of the pleasures and rewards of taking the time to do something carefully and well. Having said that, this book is a practical guide to getting things done, and so all the hand-sewing techniques shown are efficient and useful, not just lovely.

And as well as the practicalities, you'll find lots of gorgeous decorative techniques to experiment with. As you move on from basic sewing, you'll want to start developing and customizing your projects, and the chapters on embellishments (see pages 72–85) and fabric manipulation (see pages 86–99) are there to help you do just that. Do practice unfamiliar skills on scraps of fabric before launching into a project, and spend a little time working out how you are going to incorporate your new favorite technique into your most-loved TNT pattern, and then, go for it! To encourage you, at the back of the book you'll find six projects that use a variety of techniques to create simple yet stylish items for you, your friends, and your home.

Since I wrote **Me and My...** sewing has become "a thing", and about time, too! It's a fabulous occupation/obsession/pastime/hobby, and I hope that **Me and My Sewing Adventure** will help you love it as much as I do.

Kate Haxell

My sewing machines

Your very first sewing machine will probably be quite a basic model, but then you'll want to upgrade, and then you might see an irresistible bargain in a sewing machine sale, and then you spot a fabulous vintage machine in a thrift store, and before you know it, you'll have a collection of sewing machines...

Why use a vintage machine?

I have three sewing machines, a modest collection by the standards of some sewers. I had always owned modern machines and thought vintage ones just attractive relics, until I began reading some sewing blogs and discovered a world of vintage machine enthusiasts.

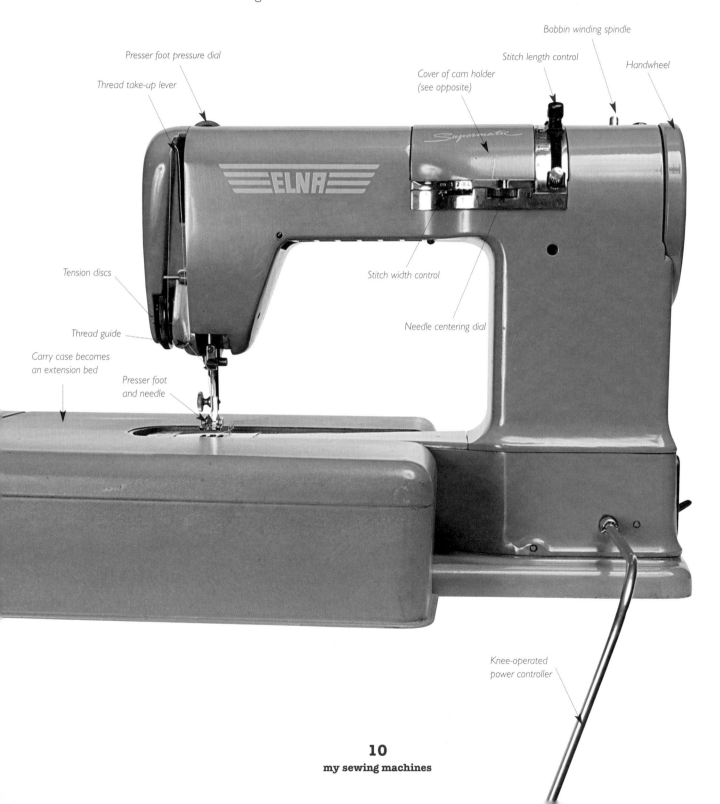

Bobbin winding spindle

Presser foot pressure dial

Stitch length control

Cover of cam holder (see opposite)

Handwheel

Thread take-up lever

Tension discs

Stitch width control

Thread guide

Needle centering dial

Carry case becomes an extension bed

Presser foot and needle

Knee-operated power controller

The "proper" reason for buying vintage is that you can get a sturdily built, great stitcher for a fraction of the price of a new machine. And it's an ecologically sound choice (if that concerns you) to continue an old machine in use. However, another reason for buying vintage—one that I consider perfectly valid—is that these machines are often gorgeous. I choose the 1956–1958 Elna Supermatic shown here mainly because I loved the color. It stitches beautifully—the straight stitch is smoother than my modern computerized machine—but I must admit that its weight is an issue and it's taken me a while to get used to the knee control, although that isn't a feature common to all vintage machines.

Choosing a vintage machine

There are many vintage machines to be had, and they vary enormously in the quality of the brand, the functions the machine offers, and the state of repair it is in, so do be prepared to do some hunting and don't just buy the first pretty machine to catch your eye. When it comes to vintage there are basically three types of machine: straight stitchers, zigzaggers, and those that can make fancy stitches, and the first thing to decide is which you want.

Straight stitchers, such as the cult-status Singer Featherweight (the name is quite misleading though), will only stitch in a straight line—but they do it brilliantly. If you own or have access to a serger or a zigzagger for overcasting raw edges, then a straight stitcher is a great buy as the tiny needle hole in the plate means that fabrics are supported close to the stitch being made and so there's less chance of irregular stitches or of fine fabrics getting pulled down into the needle hole, as is possible with the wider hole of a zigzagger. However, if you're going to have just one machine, then you should get a zigzagger so that you can finish projects properly, and work techniques such as appliqué (see page 92).

Most vintage machines that make fancy stitches use cams; these are separate plastic discs that fit onto the machine, one disc for every type of stitch: my Elna has these. A disc snaps into the housing on the top of the machine (see right), you adjust the settings as per the manual, and then it stitches a beautiful embroidery stitch. This is a bit more effort than pressing the button on my computerized machine, but not much.

Another advantage of my Elna is that it has interchangeable throat plates. This means that I can use it as a zigzagger/fancy stitcher, but swap the plate for a single-hole plate and so have the advantages of a straight stitcher.

Many big-brand vintage sewing machines will happily accept presser feet and accessories made for their younger relatives. So, if you already own a particular brand of sewing machine, it can be worth hunting for a vintage machine of the same brand because the feet you already own may well fit it.

The housing for the cams that allow the machine to sew fancy stitches.

A selection of fancy stitch cams.

Buying a vintage machine

Web auction sites will probably offer the widest, easy-to-find selection of vintage sewing machines, but there are two main drawbacks. First, you can't test the machine, and second, these machines are heavy and the shipping costs can be expensive: on occasion, more than the machine. So local thrift shops or flea markets, or adverts in local papers or on classified advert websites can be a better bet as you will see exactly what you are getting, though you will usually have to transport the machine yourself.

If you are buying from a web auction site, then don't be afraid to ask the seller lots of questions before parting with money. The photos should show front, back, both sides of the machine, and the pedal, so that you can see nothing is rusty or damaged. I like to see a video of the machine in action (so that I know it does work and isn't scarily noisy) and close-up, clear photos of all the stitches it makes. This isn't that much effort for the seller, and indeed many good sellers will have posted these things with their listing. Ask for a full list of the feet it comes with and any other accessories and attachments, and whether it has a manual: if it doesn't, many lovely sewing machine owners have posted scans of manuals on the web and you can download them for a small fee, or sometimes for free. If the machine uses cams (see page 11) and you want what they offer, then check that some come with the machine, though you can find them for sale separately if need be.

Ask how the seller is going to pack the machine for shipping; there should be a sturdy box, lots of packing material (bubble wrap, not bits of newspaper) and the pedal should be wrapped separately in the box so that there's no metal knocking against metal. Check the feedback from other people who've bought from that seller and read both the positive and negative comments. I bought my Elna from the web, did all of the above, and am completely happy with my purchase.

The essential thing to remember is that there are lots and lots of sewing machines out there: these weren't art items, they were mass-produced workhorses and lots of them have survived well. So if the machine you have your eye on looks at all suspect, then let it go and wait for another, unless you have a mechanical bent.

Caring for a vintage machine

I have only the most basic understanding of how a sewing machine (vintage or otherwise) works, and I am not interested in having any more knowledge than that. I oil my machine (as instructed in the manual), change the needle, and clean lint out of the bobbin case, and I do these things every time I start a big new project, but not if I'm just sewing a seam or two. But other than that I take my Elna to a local store for repairs or servicing, as I do with my modern machines.

However, if you have a mechanical bent there are huge resources on the web dealing with all aspects of servicing and repairing all kinds of vintage machines. Whether you want to replace the belt on a hand-crank machine, completely refurbish the table of a treadle machine, or re-wire an electric machine, there's probably some information out there. And there are a surprising variety of spare parts available from online suppliers.

Essentially, a healthy vintage machine requires no more care than a modern one, but a sickly machine can cause endless problems, and cost a lot. So if you have my disposition regarding maintenance, and the machine you are looking at buying isn't in great condition, then it's probably not the one for you.

Using a vintage machine

Sewing machines have changed very little through the years. Some older machines have a shuttle rather than the bobbin you see today, the very earliest ones produced a different type of stitch, and the thread path does vary a bit from brand to brand, but most of the vintage machines you'll find for sale today will stitch in essentially the same way as one you can buy new off the shelf.

Spend time getting used to a new-to-you machine before embarking on a project. Read the manual all the way through and test all the functions on scraps of fabric. Use different-weight fabrics and adjust the tension until you are confident that everything is working properly and that the tension is well-balanced. If anything seems amiss, it might be better to get the machine serviced before sewing with it: there's little that's more frustrating than your sewing machine chewing up an expensive fabric.

Whether you are using a vintage or a modern machine, before you start a new project always sew a few test seams on a spare piece of the project fabric. Sew through as many thicknesses as the project requires to check that the tension(s) are right and that the machine will cope with the fabric. Then get set, and sew!

Sewing machine presser feet

Most sewing machines will come with a selection of basic presser feet, and with a little ingenuity these will do almost every task you might want. However, there are lots of exciting extras you can buy that make many jobs easier to do, although some of these feet can be very expensive and so are best bought as and when you need them. These are feet available for my modern Janome sewing machine. And I've included three other sewing machine accessories that I use a lot.

Ruffler foot

This extraordinary looking item is a presser foot—honestly! It's not nearly as complicated to use as it appears, and it makes perfect, even gathers, ruffles and pleats of different depths (see page 90).

Automatic buttonhole foot

This is (obviously) only of any use if your sewing machine has an automatic buttonhole function. If it does, then you just fit the button into this foot, and it makes a buttonhole the right size (see page 62).

Walking foot

Another odd-looking thing; this foot is usually used for quilting, but because it feeds the top fabric under the needle at the same pace the feed dogs are sending the bottom fabric through, it is also great for sewing piled fabrics, such as velvet.

Blind hem foot

This foot can look quite different from brand to brand, but they all do exactly the same thing. If you really don't want to hand-sew a hem, then this foot will give you the most invisible hem stitches it is possible to make by machine.

Piping foot

This little foot holds fabric-wrapped cord in place in the grooves underneath it so that the needle will stitch along exactly the right line to make perfect piping quickly and simply (see page 76).

Overcasting foot

If you don't have a serger, this is the next best thing. This foot will help you work an overcasting stitch along the very edge of your fabric, without the fabric rolling or puckering.

Border foot

This is so simple, but so clever. When topstitching in rows or working bands of embroidery stitches (maybe as a border), line up a previous row—either to the right or left of the needle as suits—with a mark on this foot, and then sew keeping the row aligned with the mark for evenly spaced rows of stitching.

Adjustable quilting foot

This is a really useful three-in-one foot. The two black guides are removable, and without either the foot offers ⅛" (3mm) and ¼" (6mm) guide and corner marks. Fit the black guide to the outer edge for a ¼" (6mm) edge guide, or fit the other black guide to sit in the middle of the foot as a stitch-in-the-ditch guide.

Invisible zipper foot

I never use this style of zipper because I don't like the way it looks, but lots of people do like them and a foot such as this one will help you make them neatly.

Magnetic seam guide

This clamps on to the metal throat plate of your sewing machine and acts as a seam guide. Especially useful if you are sewing a seam with an allowance that is not marked on the throat plate.

Spare bobbin case

Adjusting the tension screw on the bobbin case is a last resort when adjusting the tension on a sewing machine, but something you will almost certainly need to do if you are machine embroidering using thick threads in the bobbin (see page 82). It's a good idea to keep a spare bobbin case that you can adjust for machine embroidery so that you don't risk upsetting your normal sewing tension.

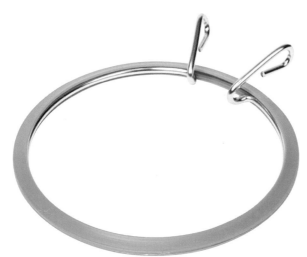

Machine embroidery hoop

Specially designed to be flat enough to slip under the needle, and with a sprung inner ring to hold fabric quickly and easily without marking it, these rings are very useful if you like using this form of embellishment (see page 82).

Useful sewing equipment

As well as the sewing basics such as scissors and tape measures, there are other bits of kit that, as your sewing skills develop, will help you do a better, and better-looking, job.

Clapper
This is a dual-purpose pressing tool; use the flat base to press steam from the iron into a seam without adding extra heat, and use the pointed tips for pressing tight corners (see pages 31 and 32).

Tailor's ham
This very firm, sawdust-filled cushion is for pressing curves over. It helps you to get the seam and seam allowances nice and flat without flattening the overall shape of the fabric (see page 31).

Point turner
Made from bamboo, this is specially designed for turning out corners and points (see page 32). Much better than poking a knitting needle or skewer through your fabric...

It's worth having two or three markers that produce different colored lines so that you can mark any color fabric.

Mechanical chalk pencil
I was really delighted to find this, a chalk pencil that makes lovely fine lines without having to sharpen it constantly. It works like a regular mechanical pencil, and the leads are available in different colors. Again, always test it to check you can remove the mark.

Fading fabric marker
This is my go-to marker, though please do always test it on a scrap of the project fabric just to check that the bright blue mark will completely disappear.

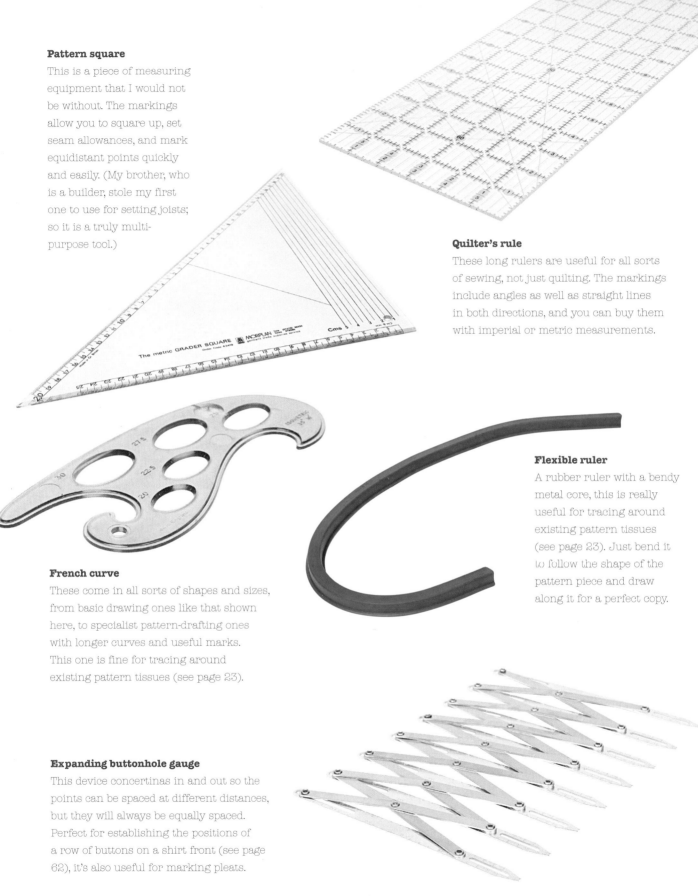

Pattern square

This is a piece of measuring equipment that I would not be without. The markings allow you to square up, set seam allowances, and mark equidistant points quickly and easily. (My brother, who is a builder, stole my first one to use for setting joists; so it is a truly multi-purpose tool.)

Quilter's rule

These long rulers are useful for all sorts of sewing, not just quilting. The markings include angles as well as straight lines in both directions, and you can buy them with imperial or metric measurements.

Flexible ruler

A rubber ruler with a bendy metal core, this is really useful for tracing around existing pattern tissues (see page 23). Just bend it to follow the shape of the pattern piece and draw along it for a perfect copy.

French curve

These come in all sorts of shapes and sizes, from basic drawing ones like that shown here, to specialist pattern-drafting ones with longer curves and useful marks. This one is fine for tracing around existing pattern tissues (see page 23).

Expanding buttonhole gauge

This device concertinas in and out so the points can be spaced at different distances, but they will always be equally spaced. Perfect for establishing the positions of a row of buttons on a shirt front (see page 62), it's also useful for marking pleats.

Silicone thimble

The metal thimble has been with us for centuries (literally). However, many sewers (including me) find them awkward, but can't do without a thimble entirely. A softer silicone thimble may be the answer. Or…

Coin thimble

A leather thimble with a metal pad for pushing the needle with might suit you. These are easy and comfortable to wear, and are my favorite.

Needle grabber

If you just require occasional help with pulling the needle through the fabric of a project, then this textured rubber disk is the answer. It makes it easy to grip the needle and pull it through thick fabric.

Pattern weights are other useful pieces of equipment that can replace pins for some functions. Turn to pages 22–25 to see how to make and use them.

Fabric clips

These mini clips are brilliant and I now use them a lot instead of pins, particularly on delicate fabrics—that pins may mark—or multiple layers of fabric that can pucker up when pinned. The bottom of the clip is flat so it doesn't catch on the bed of the sewing machine as you feed the fabric under the needle.

Before you stitch

Preparation and pressing are two of the key components of all successful sewing, even though the latter doesn't involve a needle or thread. From how you store your fabric stash (all sewers end up with a stash), to the best ways to cut out, to perfect pressing, this chapter will show you some essential skills.

Storing fabrics

All sewers end up with a fabric stash: it might be quite small—just a single box—or it may fill several cupboards. And a stash is a good thing to have, but you do need to look after it properly or when the time comes to raid it, you'll find that the fabric is useless.

The first rule is to keep all fabric out of the sun; that means behind a cupboard door, or in a light-proof box, or covered by a piece of scrap fabric. Even if you think that the sun doesn't come into your sewing space, if you keep fabric folded on open shelves, the chances are high that when you open out a length there will be sun-bleached lines along all the folded edges that were in the open.

Secondly, protect your fabrics from moths. These positively evil creatures like all natural fibers—not just wool—so use moth balls or an ecologically sound alternative in your fabric cupboards. Once in, moths can devastate a stash alarmingly quickly.

Keep your stash in some sort of order that makes sense to you so that you can actually find things in it. If you don't, you will certainly end up buying fabrics very similar to ones you already own, because your taste won't have changed. My stash fills two tall—but narrow—cupboards: one is full of cotton lengths and clear plastic boxes holding small scraps (boxed by color), and the other is full of other fabrics stored by type. Some people store their whole stash by color, others by proposed project: it doesn't matter as long as you know where to look for pieces. If you have a huge stash, creating a proper index for it is a really good idea.

Cotton fabrics can be stored folded as it's easy to iron out creases. However, fabrics that don't like the iron, or fabrics with embellishments, or with a pile, should be stored in such a way that they don't crease. The thick cardboard rolls that fabrics are wound on for sale make perfect storage—unsurprisingly! Ask your local fabric store to keep a few for you as they sell the fabric from them. Roll pile fabrics, such as velvet, onto the cardboard tube with the pile on the inside, rolling in the direction of the pile. With expensive and easily crushable silk velvets, roll a sheet of acid-free tissue paper between the layers.

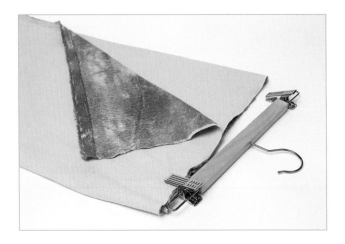

Another good way of storing pile fabrics in to hang them. Use skirt hangers to hold individual lengths, folding the fabric so that the pile is on the inside. Paint a patch of blackboard paint on the hanger then you can chalk on to it the yardage (meterage) you have of that fabric. If you have a lot of embellished or pile fabrics then you can use curtain café clips to hang them from a pole.

Hand sewing needles

There are various different types of hand sewing in this book, and having the right needle for a task can make it easier, although you don't need many needles for day-to-day types of hand sewing.

Right: sewing needles right to left—sharps size 7, sharps size 12, straw (milliners) size 7, long darner, embroidery size 5, embroidery size 10, between (quilting), curved needle.

Type of needle	Features	Sizes (the larger the number, the shorter/finer the needle)	Uses
Sharps	Medium length, sharp point, round eye, slim shaft	1–12	General sewing
Straw (milliners)	Long length, sharp point, round eye, very slim shaft	5–10	Basting fine fabrics, (see page 26), general sewing
Long darner	Very long length, sharp point, oval eye, slim shaft	1–9	Basting heavier fabrics (see page 26)
Embroidery (crewel)	Medium length, sharp point, oval eye, slim shaft	1–12	Hand embroidery (see page 83), general sewing
Between (quilting)	Short length, sharp point, round eye, very slim shaft	1–12	Quilting (see page 98), tailoring
Curved	Medium length, sharp point, oval eye, curved shaft	1½"–6" (4–15cm) long	Ladder stitch (see page 36), upholstery
Tapestry	Short length, blunt point, oval eye, thick shaft	12–28	Canvaswork, counted thread embroidery
Chenille	Short length, sharp point, oval eye, thick shaft	13–26	Hand embroidery on thicker fabrics (see page 83)
Beading	Very long length, sharp point, oval eye, very slim shaft	10–15	Bead work (see page 78)

Choose a needle with an eye large enough to carry the thread you want to use, but not so large that it leaves a hole in the fabric that is larger than the thread. You will also find that you end up with favorite needles, types, and sizes that you like to use: I have two favorites—straw size 9 for general sewing and basting, and embroidery size 10 for fiddly sewing.

Marking and cutting out fabrics

You will often want to use a pattern tissue to cut out a pattern piece from fabric. Doing this the right way will help ensure that your cut-out fabric is a precise match to the paper pattern, and so make sewing the project easier.

Making pattern weights

These weights are much better than pins for holding pattern tissues flat on fabric while you cut around them with a rotary cutter (see page 25). Using pins can rumple and distort the fabric, and can mark delicate fabrics permanently. You can buy pattern weights, but it's easy to make your own, and they will be pretty.

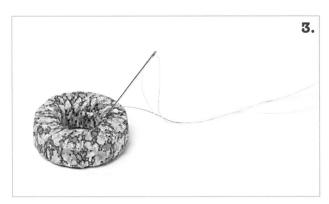
1.

1 Buy washers from a hardware store. Choose whatever size you like and buy three for each pattern weight required. Use general-purpose household adhesive to glue a stack of three washers together, aligning them neatly.

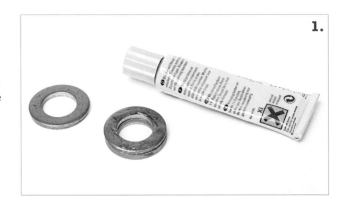
2.

2 Cut a length of bias binding; I used 20" (50cm) for each of my washer stacks. Open one side of the binding out and, starting on the inside of the washer stack, wrap the binding around the washers, overlapping the raw edge with the folded edge of the binding on each wind. Wrap right around the stack, pulling the binding as tight as possible as you wrap.

3 Once the stack is completely covered with binding, turn under the raw end on the inside of the stack. Use a needle and sewing thread to sew the end in place with whip stitches (see page 83).

3.

Food cans

You can also use regular food cans (not empty!) as pattern weights, but a couple of bloggers have complained that the prominent rim on the edge of a can left a permanent mark on their fabric. I should think that this would only be a problem with pile fabrics such as velvets, or delicate embellished fabrics, but I don't use food cans, just in case.

Tracing around pattern tissues

If you have a multi-size pattern and will want to use more than one size, or use different sizes in different areas of the garment (for example, a size 12 waist but size 14 hips), then rather than cutting out the pattern piece from the tissue it is better to trace off the lines you need onto a clean sheet of tissue. This is also useful if you are going to make fitting adjustments to a pattern, as the original will remain intact for reference if needed.

1 First, iron the original pattern with a dry iron (no steam, cool heat) to get out the creases.

2 You can buy pattern tissue paper from sewing stores and online (don't try and use wrapping paper tissue, it's too thin and will tear). Lay the pattern piece flat on a flat surface and lay a sheet of tissue over it; hold it down with pattern weights (see opposite). Use a sharp pencil and a ruler or pattern square (see page 16) to draw around the straight edges of the pattern piece.

3 Use a French curve (see page 16) to help you draw accurately around curved sections of the pattern. If you don't have a French curve, draw freehand carefully.

Vintage patterns

Tracing is also a good idea if you are working from a vintage pattern that is rather fragile and torn, or if the pattern is pristine and you would like to keep it that way. Some vintage patterns have very little in the way of construction markings, so you can add your own to a tracing.

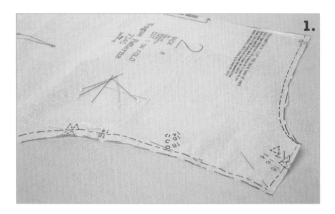

Pinning pattern tissues

If you are cutting out pattern pieces with scissors, then it's better to use pins to hold the tissue in place, as the action of the scissors will move pattern weights.

1 Smooth the tissue flat on the fabric. Put in pins with the points facing into the middle of the tissue to minimize the risk of stabbing yourself on them. If fabrics are delicate and will mark (test this on a scrap before pinning), then put in the pins along the seam line (as on the armscye here).

Card slopers

Once you have a TNT (a tried-and-tested) pattern that you love, it's better to trace it onto card to make what's called a sloper (or sometimes, a block). This sturdier version won't as easily get torn as a tissue will.

1 You can buy special dressmakers' card, but any thin card will do. Just trace off and cut out the pattern, including all darts and markings.

2 Use pattern weights to hold a sloper flat on fabric, not pins. The card is too stiff for pins and you'll just distort the fabric.

3 You can either cut around the sloper with a rotary cutter (see opposite), or draw around it with a sharp chalk pencil (see page 15) then cut it out with scissors.

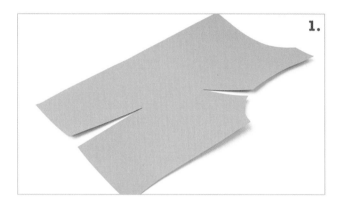

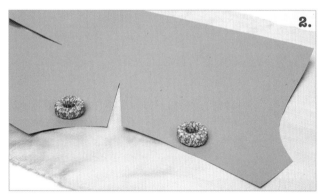

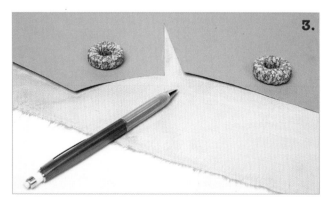

Storing patterns and slopers

Patterns are quite expensive (look out for the sales the big companies hold online), and it's worth storing them properly so that they don't get damaged, and so that you can find them easily. I keep mine by type in clear plastic mini-crates. To store slopers, punch a hole in them, thread through a string loop, and hang them up so they don't get creased.

Cutting out

Use either traditional scissors or a rotary cutter; it really is a matter of the shape you are cutting, the fabric, and personal preference.

1 Some people use rotary cutters for all cutting out. You'll need a self-healing cutting mat to protect your work surface. I use a rotary cutter and a ruler for cutting straight lines, but I struggle to cut smoothly around curves with one. Maybe I just need to practice more…

2 If you are using scissors, then do not lift the fabric more than is necessary to slide the lower blade of the scissors under it. Work the upper blade only to cut the fabric, and slide the scissors along the work smoothly to cut without creating a jagged edge.

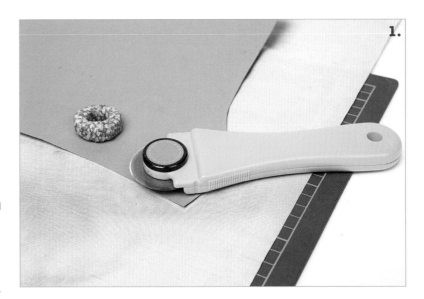

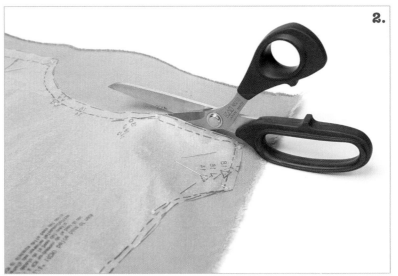

Cutting tools

I have a rotary cutter and six pairs of scissors in my workbox. I have bent-handle fabric shears, pinking shears, paper scissors, sharp embroidery scissors, old embroidery scissors, and thread snips (the latter are not strictly scissors I know, but they are what I use to cut threads when I am machine sewing). The old embroidery scissors are my all-purpose cutters, for cutting out fiddly paper templates, metal embroidery threads; anything potentially destructive.

Basting

I'm a huge fan of basting (as you'll know if you've read my previous book, *Me and My Sewing Machine*), as I find it makes for better finished items, and it really doesn't take that long. There are a few tricks and tips for basting that'll help make it really worth while to do.

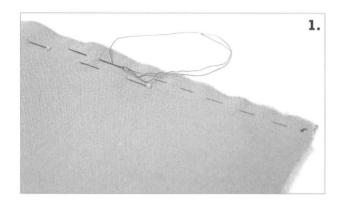

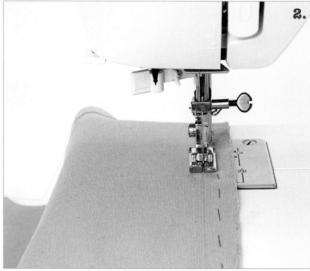

Basting seams

This is one of the most common uses of basting, along with hems. The technique is simple; it's the position of the basting stitches that makes a difference.

1 On non-slippery fabrics, use a long needle such as a straw or long darner (see page 21) to make running stitches through all layers. Work the basting stitches within the seam allowance (marked here in blue for clarity).

2 Basting within the seam allowance means that there's no danger of the basting leaving visible marks on the finished project. And when you machine-sew the seam the basting stitches won't get caught up in the machining, which can make them difficult to take out.

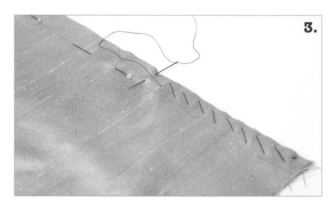

3 Slippery fabrics, or fabrics with a pile, can benefit from diagonal basting to hold the layers firmly together and prevent them "creeping" (the bottom layer moving at a different pace to the top layer) as you machine the hem. Work the stitches as shown, again within the seam allowance.

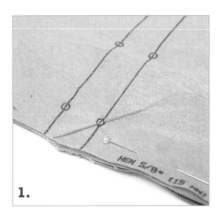

1.

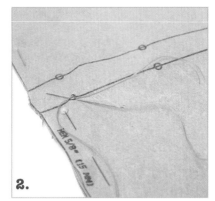

2.

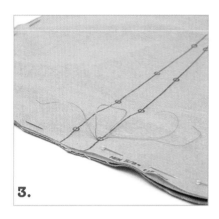

3.

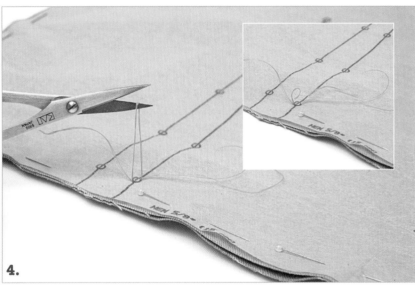

4.

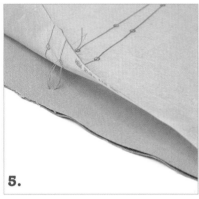

5.

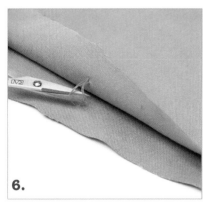

6.

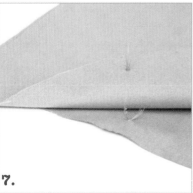

7.

Tailors' tacks

These are a traditional way of marking pattern points on fabric so that you can match them at a later stage. They might seem a bit fiddly, and aren't vital on simple patterns, but they will help you when making up more complex projects. Work tailors' tacks once the pattern pieces are all cut out, but before taking the tissues off the fabric.

1 Thread a sewing needle (see page 21) with a long, doubled length of sewing thread. Make a small stitch through the tissue and fabric at the marked point on the pattern piece, making sure you stitch through all layers. Leave a 2" (5cm) tail of thread.

2 Make a second stitch in the same way at the same point.

3 Pull the thread through, leaving a 2" (5cm) long loop. Cut the thread, leaving a 2" (5cm) tail.

4 Cut the loop of thread, leaving small tufts. Repeat Steps 1–3 at all points that need to be marked.

5 Take out any pins and carefully lift the tissue off the fabric and tufts.

6 Separate the layers of fabric just a little and use embroidery scissors to snip through the tufts between them.

7 Each layer of fabric is marked in an identical position with tufts of thread.

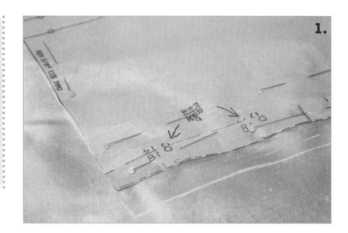

Thread tracing

This is a very useful technique for marking seamlines on pattern pieces where you will need to refer to them again, but don't want to risk using a fabric marker (see page 15). Work it on a single layer of fabric while the pattern tissue is still pinned in position.

1 Fold back the pattern tissue along the seamline to be marked. Pin it in place.

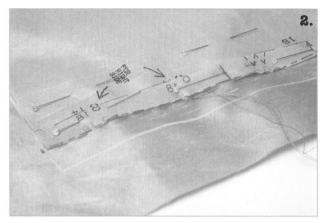

2 Using a long, fine needle (see page 21), work a line of long running stitches along the folded edge of the tissue, following the relevant seamline.

3 Remove the tissue and the seamline is marked on the fabric.

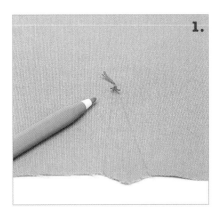

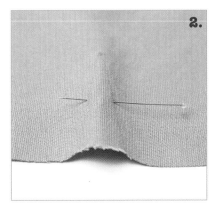

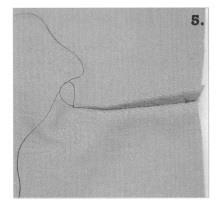

Darts

There is more than one way of marking a dart, but this is my preferred method.

1 Make a tailors' tack (see page 27) at the point of the dart. Once the tissue is removed, use a fabric marker (see page 15) and ruler to draw lines, on the wrong side of the fabric, from the tack to the dart points at the edge of the fabric. (If your pattern does not have dart points, then just cut your own at the top of each dart as you cut out the pattern piece.)

2 Take out the tailors' tack. Put a pin through the drawn, lines, as shown. Press the dart together along the pin, so that the drawn lines match up.

3 Put a pin in the dart to hold it in place.

4 From the top of the dart, machine along the drawn line to the point. Do not reverse stitches at either end.

5 Firmly knot the threads at each end of the dart. Press the dart to one side.

Pressing

After a needle and thread, the single most important tool in sewing is your iron. Good pressing can make all the difference to a project, and it's so easy to do.

Pressing a straight seam

There are two stages to pressing any seam, and doing both does make a difference.

1 First press the line of stitching. This helps "set" the stitches and makes them sink into the fabric.

2 Then press the seam either open or to one side, as desired. If necessary (test on a scrap of fabric to check), to prevent marks from the edges of the seam allowances showing through on the right side of the fabric, place a strip of paper under each seam allowance before pressing. I use brown parcel paper, but any paper without ink on it should be fine.

Pressing a shaped seam

Once you have sewn a shaped seam (see page 41), or a curved seam, you need to press it carefully to ensure that the work you have put into creating the curves isn't simply pressed flat. Start by pressing the stitching flat, as for a straight seam (see above).

Place the seam over a tailors' ham (see page 15), adjusting it so that the curve of the seam is supported by a curve of the ham, then press the seam open carefully, pressing each notched section apart smoothly along the entire seam.

Using pressing cloths

A pressing cloth has two functions: to prevent the hot plate of the iron directly touching the fabric and, when dampened, to force steam into the fabric to help shape it or flatten it, as needed.

1 My favorite pressing cloth is an old cotton tea towel with all the hems cut off with pinking shears. The thick, absorbent cotton tea-towel fabric holds plenty of water, making it a great damp pressing cloth. Make sure that any towel you use has been washed several times to remove any surface treatment and ensure that, if it has a pattern, no color will run.

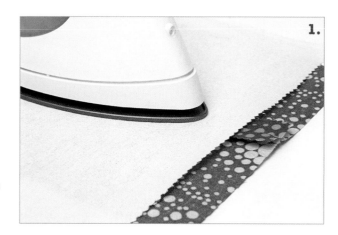

2 For pressing areas where you need to be able to see the fabric you are working on, use a square of silk organza as a pressing cloth. Indeed, some sewers prefer this fabric as a pressing cloth at all times. For neatness, it's better to fray back the edges of this fabric than to pink them.

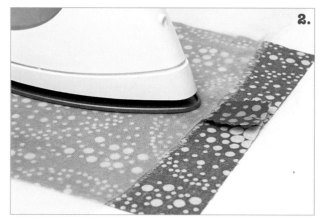

Using a clapper

This wooden gadget might look a bit odd (see page 15 for a photograph of the whole of a clapper), and they are quite expensive, but if you are going to do a lot of sewing then a clapper is a good tool and so a good investment.

When you are concerned that the seam allowances will make a mark on the right side of the fabric after you have pressed a seam, use a clapper. Hold the iron just above the seam, without touching the fabric, and press the steam button to send a jet of steam into the fabric. Immediately press down on the seam with the clapper, forcing the steam right into the fabric and pressing it flat at the same time.

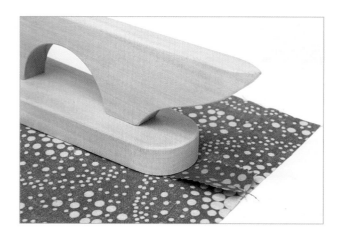

1.

2.

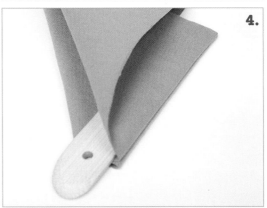

3.

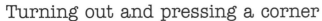

Turning out and pressing a corner

Show a project to a keen seamstress and if there are any corners, she will immediately inspect both sides of them. A neat corner is an indicator of good sewing, and here's how to make one using a point turner (see page 15).

1 Machine-sew the corner seams.

2 Using scissors, trim the seam allowances. Trim at a shallow angle toward the corner, then cut the tip of the corner off completely, about ⅛" (3mm) from the stitching.

3 Lay an edge of the point turner against one seam, tucking it between the seam allowances so that it's right up against the stitching, with the point against the corner itself.

4 Fold the fabric smoothly over the point turner, so that it ends up inside the corner. Wriggle the turner gently to ease the point of the corner completely square.

5 Slip the turned corner over a point on the top of the clapper to press it perfectly.

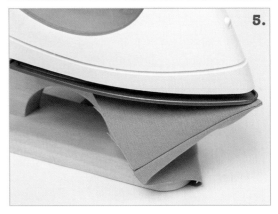

4.

5.

Hand utility stitches

These are the hand-sewing stitches you'll need to know to create and finish projects by hand. They are simple stitches, but made neatly and well they are both practical and good-looking: always a winning combination. Stitches are worked from right to left across the fabric unless otherwise stated.

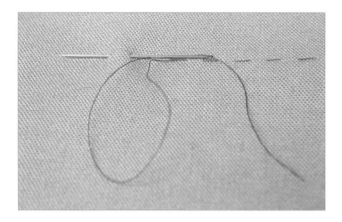

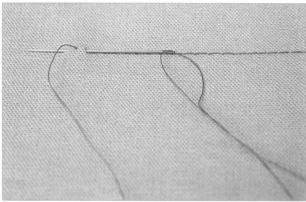

Running stitch

The simplest of all hand stitches, this can also be used as a decorative embroidery stitch (see below right).

Use a long needle (see page 21), and make small stitches in and out of the fabric. Keep the stitches neat and even if they are going to be seen, but no need to worry if you are basting; just stitch quickly!

Backstitch

This is a stitch to use for hand-sewing a seam (see page 47).

Bring the needle up through the fabric. *Insert it a stitch length behind where it came out and bring it out a stitch length in front, as shown. Repeat from * to make a continuous, firm line of stitching.

Utility as embroidery

There is a rich tradition of utility stitches as decoration, from the simple aesthetics of naïve or folk art, to the urban style of deliberate distressing, to the contemporary vintage-inspired principles of "visible mending". Running stitch and backstitch are as much used for embroidery as they are for making, and herringbone stitch (see page 35) is beautifully decorative as well as perfectly practical.

Pick stitch

A more discreet version of backstitch that can be used when the stitches will be visible (see page 68).

Bring the needle up through the fabric. *Insert it a tiny distance behind where it came out and bring it out a stitch length in front, as shown. Repeat from * to make a dotted line of stitching.

Slip stitch

This is probably the best-known hemming stitch, and indeed the term "slip stitch" is often used as a generic when what is actually needed is fell stitch (see below), or ladder stitch (see page 36). Slip stitch makes a neat, firm hem.

1 Fold up the hem as required. At the right-hand end, bring the needle up through the upper folded edge. *Make a tiny stitch through the main fabric, as shown, picking up just a couple of threads so that the stitch barely shows on the right side.

2 Make a stitch through the hem, slipping the needle along the fold. Repeat from * to sew the hem.

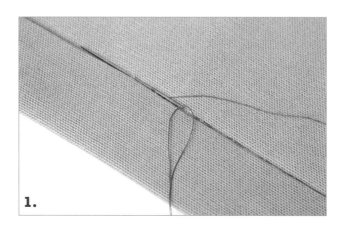

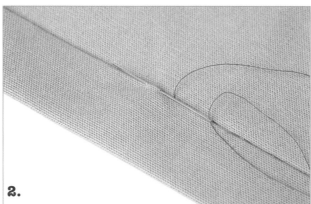

Fell stitch

This is similar in principle to slip stitch, but the visible stitches are straight and neat, making it suitable for visible hems (see page 57). It's shown this way up to make it easier for you to see what's happening.

Fold up the hem as required. At the left-hand end, bring the needle up through the hem, very close to the folded edge. *Make a tiny stitch through the main fabric immediately above where the thread came out, as shown, picking up just a couple of threads so that the stitch barely shows on the right side. Take the needle at an angle through the hem, so that it comes out very close to the folded edge. Repeat from * to sew the hem.

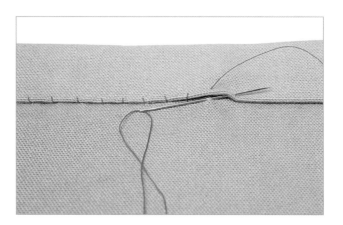

Herringbone stitch

This is a very stable, strong hemming stitch. The needle points right to left, but don't let that confuse you; the stitch is, unusually, worked from left to right.

1 Fold up the hem as required. At the left-hand end, bring the needle up through the folded edge. *Right to left, make a tiny stitch through the main fabric, as shown, picking up just a couple of threads so that the stitch barely shows on the right side.

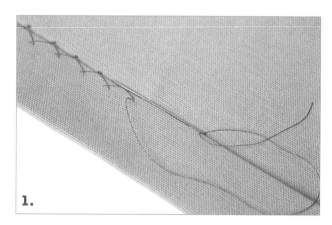

2 Take the needle across to the right a stitch length and, from right to left, make a stitch through the folded hem. This can be deeper and longer than the main fabric stitch if preferred. Take the needle across to the right a stitch length and repeat from * to sew the hem.

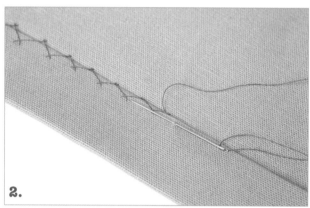

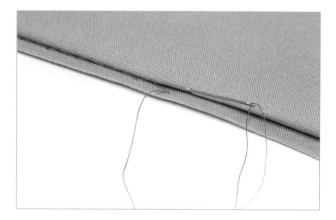

Catch stitch

This is herringbone stitch (see above), worked inside the hem so that it is invisible on both the right and wrong sides. Use this where the inside of the hem might show.

Fold up the hem as required. Lay the fabric wrong side down, then fold it back so that you can see the top edge of the folded hem allowance. Work herringbone stitch along this edge, taking the needle through the inner layer only of the folded hem.

Whip stitch

A fast-to-sew stitch that makes neat, strong seams, this can be worked on the right side, as here (see also page 47), or on the wrong side (see page 94).

    Turn under the seam allowance of both edges to be joined and place them together. *Take the needle straight through both pieces, a very short distance from the folded edge. From the same side, repeat from *, as shown, so that the thread wraps around the folded edges.

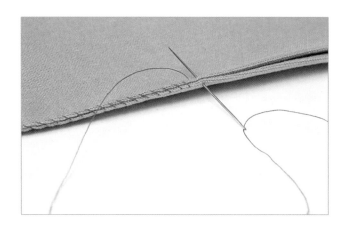

Ladder stitch

This is used to sew up a gap in a machine-sewn seam.

1 Press under the seam allowances across the gap to be sewn up. From the inside, bring the needle up through the pressed fold. *Taking the needle straight across to the opposite folded edge, make a small stitch along the fold, as shown. The more accurately the stitch follows the fold, the neater the seam will be.

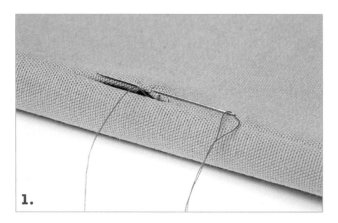

2 Take the needle straight across to the first folded edge and make a stitch along that fold. Repeat from *, making sure that the stitches all run straight from one edge to the other, so they look like the rungs of a ladder. Pull the stitches taut but not tight, or the edge will pucker.

Buttonhole stitch

Used for making hand-stitched buttonholes (see page 63), when worked with the stitches spaced further apart this becomes a decorative embroidery stitch known as blanket stitch (see below).

Start by bringing the thread through from the wrong side of the fabric, then make a tiny stitch to take the needle back through to the wrong side. *Before pulling the needle and thread through, loop the working thread under the point of the needle, as shown. Pull the needle through. From the front, make another tiny stitch through to the wrong side, very close to the last stitch, and repeat from *.

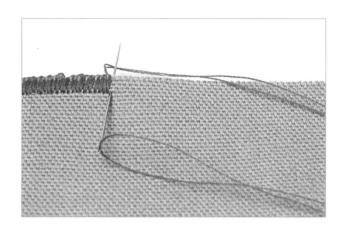

Blanket stitch

So called because it is traditionally used to edge blankets, this is a versatile and decorative embroidery stitch. You can work it evenly and neatly, or with different-length legs as shown here (see also page 117), or with the legs spaced at different intervals. It can run in straght lines, curve elegantly, or form small wheels.

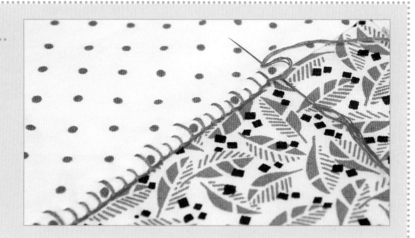

Starting and finishing stitching

You can start a line of stitching with either a firm knot or a couple of small backstitches in a discreet spot. Some sewers think that knots might come undone, or leave a visible bump, while others think that tiny stitches are not very secure; so choose whichever method you prefer, or that suits the task in hand.

To finish a line of stitching, make a single backstitch and pull the needle through, leaving a small loop of thread, as shown. Take the needle through the loop and then pull tight. Repeat, then trim off the excess thread.

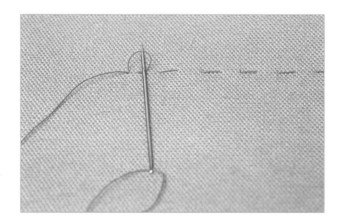

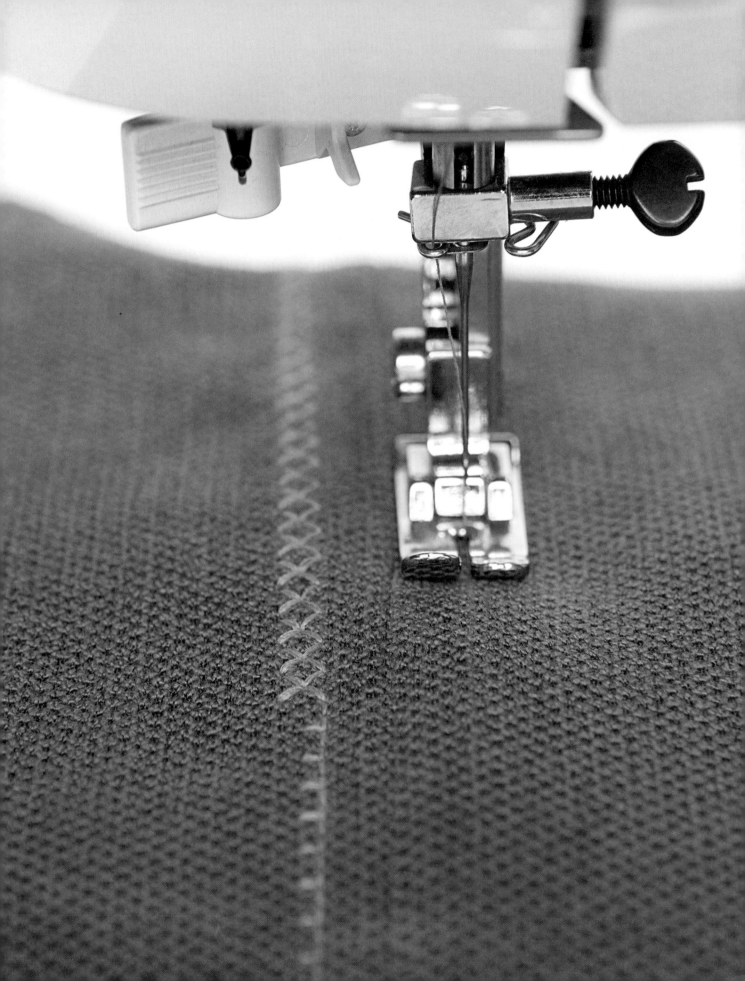

Seams
to sew

A seam is probably the most common element in sewing: almost every project has a seam or two. Well-made, pattern-matched seams can give a simple project an elegant touch, and they aren't difficult to sew.

Pattern matching across a seam

This is a technique most often used for soft furnishings such as drapes, where a mismatch in the pattern either side of a seam would be very noticeable. However, keen clothes-makers often pattern-match straight garment seams, especially with bold patterns and at obvious seams—such as center back—and this does give a garment a stylish touch.

Check out...
Pressing, page 30

Best used for...
All fabrics
Straight seams on fabrics with an obvious pattern

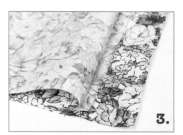

1 Start by establishing the pattern repeat (see Pattern Repeat, below right), then cut the required lengths of fabric from the same point in the repeat. Press under a ⅝" (1.5cm) seam allowance on one of the pieces to be seamed.

2 Lay the folded edge on the other piece of fabric and position it so that the pattern matches across the fold. Pin the folded edge in place, pinning accurately and as close to the fold as possible.

3 Fold the main part of the upper piece of fabric over onto the underlying piece (so the two pieces are right-sides together), exposing the pressed-under seam allowance and the excess fabric of the underlying piece.

4 Pin the fabrics together along the exposed seam allowance.

5 Remove the pins inserted in Step 2 so that you are left simply with two pieces of fabric pinned right sides together. Trim the excess fabric of the underlying piece to match the seam allowance of the upper piece.

6 Position the fabric under the foot of the sewing machine so that the needle will start sewing along the pressed line: you can check this by turning the handwheel to lower the needle until it just touches the fabric. Machine-sew along the pressed line, then press the seam open.

Above: a perfectly pattern-matched seam is almost invisible.

Pattern repeat

This is the distance between repeating motifs in a pattern. Find a prominent feature and put a pin in the fabric, then look down the length for the same feature again, and put in another pin. The distance between the pins is the pattern repeat. To match a pattern you need to add the length of the repeat to each length you are going to cut.

Shaped seam

This will usually be a princess seam, where an inward curving edge needs to be sewn to an outward curving edge. Shaped seams are a bit fiddly to sew, but making them well will allow you to make fitted garments that lie smoothly without puckering in the seams.

Check out...
Pressing, page 30

Best used for...
Light and mediumweight fabrics

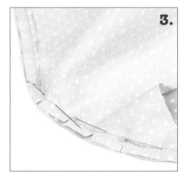

1 Set the sewing machine to a medium straight stitch and stay stitch both edges to be seamed, stitching inside the inside seam allowance. If you have always skipped stay stitching because it doesn't seem that important, please don't skip it here; it will make a difference to your finished seam (see Step 3).

2 Using the tips of dressmaking scissors, clip the edges of the inward curving piece up to the stay stitching. Make the clips about 1" (2.5cm) apart.

3 Pin the two pieces together, easing them gently to fit. This is where the stay stitching comes in as without it the curving edges will undoubtedly get stretched and then your seam will never lie flat.

4 Machine-sew the seam, sewing slowly and carefully and easing the fabric as you go to avoid trapping puckers in the stitching.

5 Again using the tips of dressmaking scissors, cut small V-shaped notches in the outward curving seam allowance, cutting through the stay stitching to within ⅛" (3mm) of the seam stitching. Position the notches between the clips in the other seam allowance to avoid any weak spots in the seam. Press the seam open over a tailor's ham.

Above: a smoothly curving seam with no puckers is what you are aiming for.

Lapped seam

This is an effective method of joining by hand a gathered and a flat piece of fabric, each of different weights. Here, it's a mediumweight chenille fabric and a lightweight cotton, but any combination can be successfully and neatly joined. It's an ideal technique for attaching a diaphanous gathered skirt to a fitted bodice.

Check out...

Pressing, page 30
Running stitch, page 33
Fell stitch, page 34

Best used for...

Joining fabrics of
    different weights

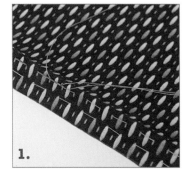

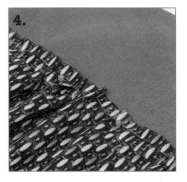

Above: the gathers are not crushed or bunched as they can be if the seam is machine-sewn.

1 Press under ⅝" (1.5cm) seam allowance along the top edge of the piece of fabric to be gathered. Open it out and work two rows of running stitch within the seam allowance (see Gathering, right). Alternatively, machine two rows of long straight stitch with a very loose stitch tension. Knot the ends of the threads together.

2 Pull up the gathers to the desired width.

3 On the flat piece of fabric, press under ⅝" (1.5cm) seam allowance on the edge to be seamed. Lay this piece flat, right side down.

4 Lay the gathered piece right side down on top of the flat piece, matching the pressed seamlines. Pin it in place, making sure that the gathers are evenly spaced.

5 On the right side, sew the pieces together using fell stitch. If necessary, ease the gathers as you sew to ensure that they lie neatly.

Gathering

To make neat, even gathers, you need to work two rows of running stitch about ¼" (6mm) apart, matching the stitches so the two rows look the same. They don't have to match perfectly, but if they are very different the gathers will be flatter and less even. If you use a sewing machine the gathers will usually be smaller than if hand-sewn, and do remember to re-set the stitch tension afterwards.

Topstitched seam

With thick fabrics, topstitching prevents the seam allowances rolling and so the seams will lie flatter. Plus, the visible line of stitching adds detail that is especially suited to more tailored projects. If your sewing machine will work fancy embroidery stitches, then you can topstitch with one of those for a decorative finish. If you are doing this, then sew a sample of the stitch on a piece of scrap fabric, measure the width of it, and if necessary adjust the width of the seam allowances so that the topstitching lies within them.

Check out...
Pressing, page 30
Machine embroidery stitches,
    page 58

Best used for...
Thick and mediumweight
    fabrics

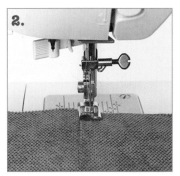

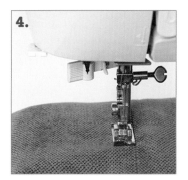

1 Sew the seam taking a standard ⅝" (1.5cm) seam allowance. With thick fabrics press the seam open. With thinner fabrics you can either press the seam open if you want topstitching on both sides of the seam, or press both seam allowances to one side if you only want topstitching on one side. If the fabric doesn't press flat easily, you may want to consider basting the seam allowances before topstitching to ensure that they stay flat and smooth.

2 Right-side up, position the fabric in the sewing machine so that the left-hand edge of the presser foot runs along the seam.

3 Sew the line of topstitching, making sure that the presser foot stays against the seam so that the line is straight.

4 Going back to the same end of the seam, position the presser foot with the right-hand edge against the seam and topstitch the other seam allowance. Stitching from the same end both times helps prevent the seam distorting and puckering.

5 If you are using a fancy embroidery stitch, you may need to topstitch further away from the seam to ensure that the stitch doesn't run over it; you might find a quilting guide useful to help you keep the stitch in a straight line.

Above: topstitching can be a simple straight line (left), or a decorative machine embroidery stitch (right).

Above: the line of stitching will show between motifs, but the uninterrupted pattern still looks great.

Lace appliqué seam

This technique is a bit time-consuming, but does make a very attractive seam on lace as the pattern is uninterrupted. You can use the same principle to seam printed fabric if it has a reasonably bold pattern, turning under the cut edge and stitching it as for turned-edge appliqué (see page 92).

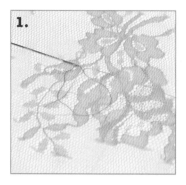

1.

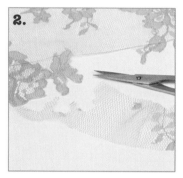

2.

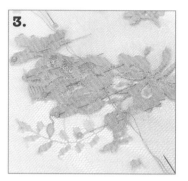

3.

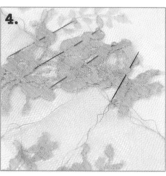

4.

5.

Check out...

Tailors' tacks, page 27

Thread tracing, page 28

Fell stitch, page 34

Pattern matching across a
    seam, page 40

Best used for...

Lace fabrics

1 Establish the pattern match in the lace (see Matching Lace Patterns, right). Thread trace the seamlines of both pieces, making the seam allowances wide enough to fit at least one whole lace motif. Lay the pieces flat and overlap them so the seamlines and the pattern match, and check you are happy with how it all looks.

2 Separate the pieces and set one aside. Cut along the traced seamline on the other piece, cutting straight along it between motifs, but cutting carefully around the edges of the motifs. Try not to cut the thread tracing as it will still be useful, but if you do, don't worry about it, just leave the threads in place.

3 Lay the cut piece back on top of the uncut piece, matching the seamlines and pattern as in Step 1. Pin the pieces together, pinning the overlapping motifs carefully so that they match perfectly.

Matching lace patterns

As lace is translucent it is easy to match patterns. Overlap the pieces at the approximate position of the seamline, and adjust them until the motifs overlap perfectly. Use a tailor's tack to mark the spot to start the thread tracing. As you cut around motifs, cut off thin elements, such as the leafy stems here, and have those on the underlying layer only.

4 Using matching sewing thread, fell stitch the pieces together, stitching around the edges of motifs and along the traced seamline between them. Take out the pins and thread tracings.

5 Fold the upper piece of fabric over the underlying piece, exposing the uncut seam allowance on the underlying piece. Trim this to about ¼" (6mm).

Stabilizing seams

This is a very useful technique that is especially applicable to making clothes. Use it to create firm shoulder seams in garments made from knit and any other fabric with even the smallest amount of stretch; never again will you have unevenly drooping shoulders after just a couple of washes of a shirt that took you ages to make.

Check out...
Basting, page 26

Best used for...
Knit and other stretch fabrics

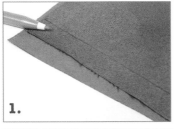

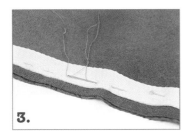

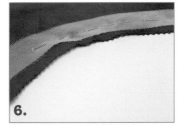

Straight seam

Use this technique for a straight seam, such as a shoulder seam.

1 Using a fading fabric marker and a ruler, draw the seam line on the wrong side of one of the pieces to be joined.

2 Cut a piece of twill tape (see Tapes, right) to length. Place the fabrics right sides together and pin the tape over the seamline, pinning the fabrics together at the same time.

3 Baste along the outer edge of the tape to hold all the layers together within the seam allowance.

4 Machine-sew the seam: it would be worth doing a test seam with scraps of fabric and tape as you will be sewing through three layers.

Curved seam

If the seam you want to stabilize is curved, then you need the stabilizer to be similarly curved.

5 Cut a bias strip of silk organza the required length. Hold the ends and stretch the fabric firmly. Iron it, stretching it at the same time. This should eliminate any stretch from the strip, but still allow it to ease around a gentle curve.

6 Pin and baste, then sew the strip to the seamline just as for a straight seam.

Right: the tape (top), or selvage (bottom), is only visible on the wrong side of the seam.

Tapes

Twill tape is a herringbone weave, which makes it stable. It can be a bit chunky for lighter fabrics, so use hem tape instead. You can also use selvages of cotton fabrics. A selvage is more tightly woven than the main fabric, and neatly trimmed-off selvages are stable and can look pretty: they may only ever be seen by you, but you deserve a good-looking treat.

Bound seam

Finishing the edges of seam allowances with dedicated seam binding is practical because it prevents fraying without adding bulk (useful with thick fabrics), and it gives a couture-style finish that's well worth the effort if the inside of the project will be visible, such as with an unlined jacket. Choose a rayon seam binding tape for the smoothest, least bulky finish, though you can use cotton bias binding; just iron it open and flat before starting. This method requires two lines of stitching, but does produce the best results by far.

Check out...
Pressing, page 30

Best used for...
Thick fabrics
Fabrics that fray easily

Above: seam binding can tone with or match the fabric (right), or be in an accent or contrast color for added detail (left).

1 Sew the seam taking a standard ⅝" (1.5cm) seam allowance and press the seam open. Unwind a length of the seam binding from the spool, but do not cut it. Starting about ¾" (2cm) from the end of the binding, pin it to the wrong side of one seam allowance, with about one-third of the width of the binding on the fabric. If the fabric is slippery, it's best to pin the binding in place right along the seam allowance, but with practice you will be able to position and sew the binding without pinning.

2 Set the sewing machine to a medium straight stitch. Fold the other seam allowance to the left so that it's lying against the main fabric and position the fabric in the sewing machine so that the needle will start sewing very close to the edge of the seam binding. Sew the binding to the fabric right along the seam allowance, taking out pins as you go. At the other end, cut the binding leaving a ¾" (2cm) loose end.

3 Sew binding to the wrong side of the other seam allowance in exactly the same way.

4 On each seam allowance fold the binding over the edge of the fabric, encasing the raw edge, and iron it. Rayon binding irons beautifully, so you won't need to pin the loose edge in place on the right side of the fabric.

5 Right side up, position one seam allowance in the sewing machine so that the needle will start sewing very close to the edge of the binding: you can check this by turning the handwheel to lower the needle until it just touches the fabric. Sew the loose edge in place to finish binding the seam. Press the seam flat again.

Hand-sewn seams

Since sewing machines became easily available domestic items, seams are rarely sewn by hand. However, hand sewing is a great way of negotiating tricky corners or sections of a seam, even if the rest of it is machine-sewn. And some sewers love hand sewing and happily sit with their work in their laps, stitching peacefully and rhythmically along all their seams.

Check out...
Sewing needles, page 21
Pressing, page 30
Hand utility stitches, page 33

Best used for...
Lightweight and mediumweight
    fabrics

Backstitch seam

This is the hand-sewn version of a machined seam.

1 Using a fading fabric marker and a ruler, draw the seam line on the wrong side of one of the pieces of fabric to be joined.

2 Pin the pieces right sides together. Using single sewing thread and a suitable needle, backstitch along the marked line.

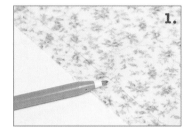

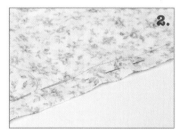

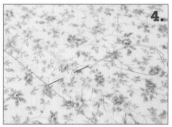

3 Press the seam allowances to one side, rather than pressing them open.

4 Whip stitch the raw edges of the seam allowances, making quite large stitches. Do not pull the stitches tight as this will pucker the seam allowances and they'll show on the right side when the seam is ironed.

Above: a whip stitched seam (top) and a backstitched seam (bottom).

Whip stitch seam

With this seam the stitches show on the right side, which can be a feature; or reserve it for quick, fun makes, such as fancy dress costumes.

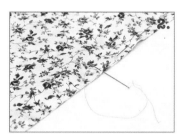

1 Press under the seam allowances on both pieces to be joined.

2 Pin the pieces wrong sides together, matching the pressed seam lines exactly. Whip stitch along the seam.

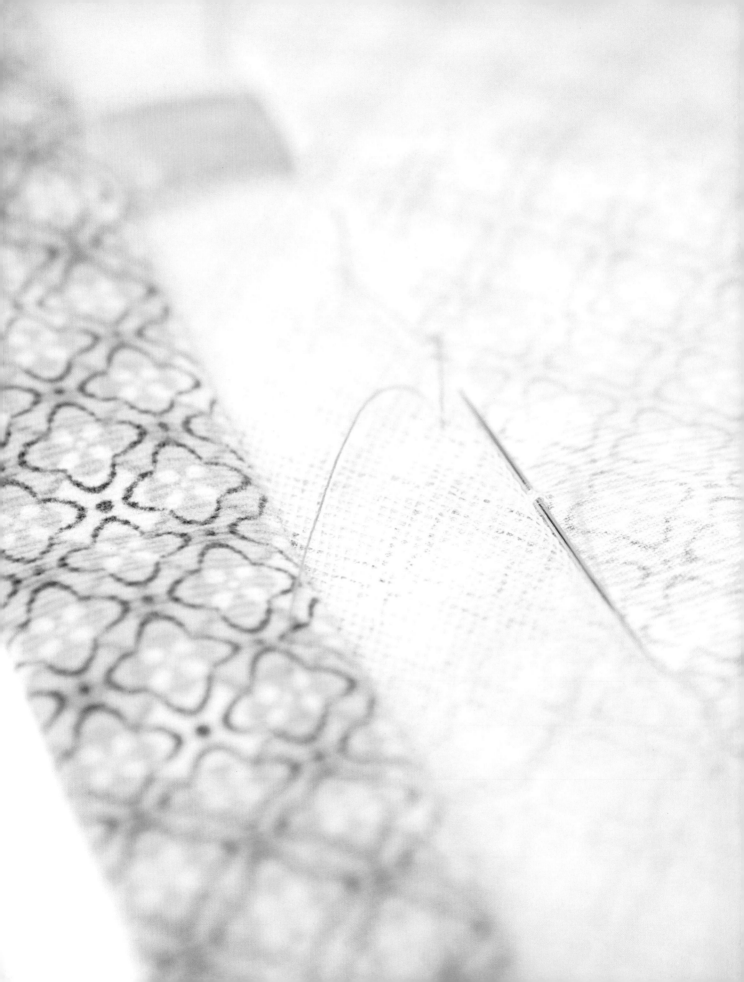

Hems to turn up

Stepping beyond a simple machined hem allows you to add couture-style touches to garments of all sorts. Whether it's a pretty detail that'll be glimpsed as you move, or a structural element that will help shape your project, hems have a lot to offer beyond a change of length.

Preparing a garment hem

Before you actually sew a hem you need to establish the height of it and make sure that it is even along its length, and that takes a little preparation, and—if the garment is for you—a friend.

The first thing to do is to leave the garment to hang for a day or so to let the fabric settle. If any part of the project is cut on the bias (for example, the hem of a circle skirt), then you should hang the project for at least a week—preferably two—as the fabric can drop quite a bit, resulting in an uneven edge. If you just hem straightaway, in a couple of weeks the edge of the garment will be very wobbly indeed.

Suspend the project by the top edge (so for a skirt, clip the waistband into a skirt hanger) and just hang it in your closet and ignore it for a while.

Turning up a hem

Once you are ready to start making the hem, you'll need a ruler and pins, and be prepared to crawl around on your knees. If the garment is for you, then this is where you need a friend.

1 You should measure a hem height up from the floor on the person who the garment is for. Don't measure down from the waist, because the curves of the body will fill out the garment to different degrees in different areas below the waist. I have a vintage hem-measuring stick (shown here), but a ruler will work just as well. Stand the ruler straight up on end on the floor and establish the height you want the hem to be. Put in a pin to mark that height at center front, center back, and each side seam. Then turn up the hem to the marked point and pin it, putting in the pins vertically with the points facing up. Using the ruler as before, pin up the hem all around.

2 Once the hem is pinned and you are happy with the length, cut off any excess as required (do decide on the style of hem you want to use first and check what hem allowance you need for it). Then baste the hem in place (see page 26), stitching halfway between the lower and upper edges all around.

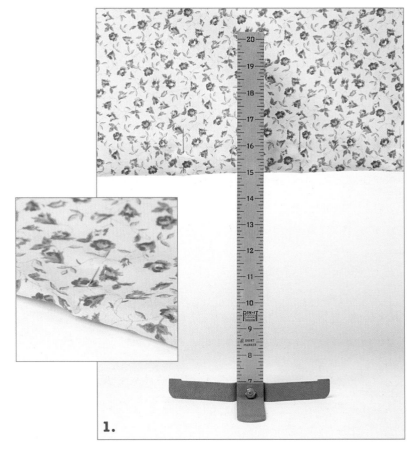

1.

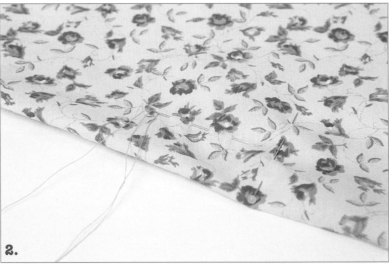

2.

Interfaced invisible hem

Above: an interfaced hem on the right side of a project (right), and on the wrong side (left).

This hem is invisible on the right side, but a small amount of interfacing shows on the wrong side, so it is best used where there will be a lining. The interfacing will add a little body to the hem.

Check out...
Pressing, page 30
Slip stitch, page 34

Best used for...
All fabrics
Where a lining will cover the
    wrong side of the hem

1 Press under a double hem; here it is ⅜" (1cm) then 1" (2.5cm).

2 Using pinking shears or a rotary cutter with pinking blade, cut a strip of lightweight fusible interfacing to the width you want and the length of the hem—or several pieces that add up to that length (see Cutting the Interfacing, below right).

3 Fold open the second hem. Position the interfacing on the wrong side of the fabric so that when the hem is folded up again, about ⅜" (1cm) of interfacing shows above the hem. Check that the interfacing is correctly positioned, then iron it in place. If you are using several pieces, then just butt them up to one another; don't overlap them.

4 Slip stitch the hem, catching the interfacing only, not the main fabric, in the upper stitches.

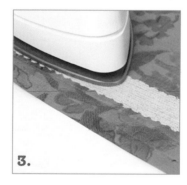

1.

2.

3.

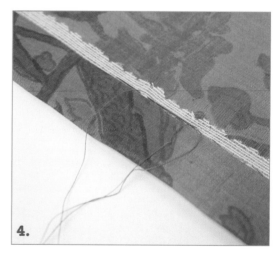

4.

Cutting the interfacing

If you want to add more body to the hem, then cut the strip the full depth of the second hem plus ⅜" (1cm)—so here it would be 1⅜" (3.5cm). If you want minimal added body, then cut the strip ¾" (2cm) wide, which is what I have done here. Do test the fusible interfacing on a scrap of the fabric first to check that it doesn't leave an impression.

Curved hem

Above: a deeply curved hem on the right side of a project (right), and on the wrong side (left).

For a deeply curved or shaped hem, this is the best technique. It isn't attractive on the wrong side, so it's best to have a lining to cover that.

Check out...

Basting, page 26
Thread tracing, page 28
Pressing, page 30
Slip stitch, page 34

Best used for...

A deeply curved hem
Lightweight and mediumweight fabrics
Where a lining will cover the wrong side of the hem

1 Serge or zigzag stitch the raw edge of the fabric.

2 Thread trace the hemline: here it's been marked with a chalk pencil on the wrong side first.

3 Fold up the hem along the thread tracing and press just the fold. Concentrate on pressing a smooth hemline, and be careful not to press any of the ripples in the hem allowance flat.

4 Pin the hem in place, putting in vertical pins 1" (2.5cm) apart, and allowing ripples of fabric to form between them. Keep the pins and ripples at right angles to the hemline.

5 Baste along the top edge of the hem allowance, stitching between the ripples and not flattening them. Take out the pins.

6 Slip stitch the hem, again stitching between the ripples. Take out the basting stitches.

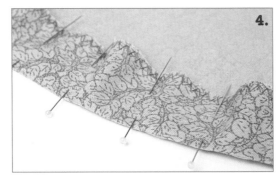
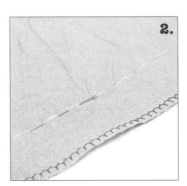

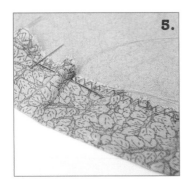
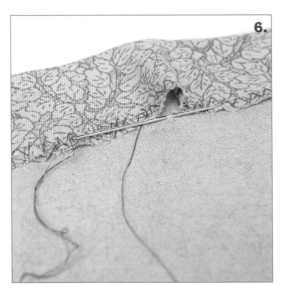

Bias-faced hem

Above: a bias-faced hem on the right side of a project (right), and on the wrong side (left).

For a hem with a shallow curve you can use this technique, which has the advantage of looking good on both sides. You can cut the bias strip from the project fabric, or use a contrast for added detail (as here). This is a narrow hem, so start by trimming the hem allowance to ⅝" (1.5cm).

1.

2.

3.

4.

5.

6.

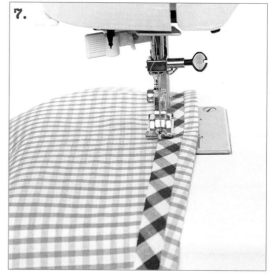

7.

Check out...

Pressing, page 30
Topstitched seam, page 43

Best used for...

A shallow curved hem
Lightweight and mediumweight
    fabrics
Where the wrong side of the
    hem might show

1 Cut bias strips of fabric measuring the required depth of the facing plus ⅝" (1.5cm). Join the strips to form a continuous strip that is the length of the hem.

2 Press under ⅜" (1cm) to the wrong side along one edge of the strip.

3 Right sides together, pin the raw edge of the strip to the raw edge of the fabric.

4 Set the sewing machine to a medium straight stitch and sew the pieces together taking a ¼" (6mm) seam allowance.

5 Lay the fabric right side down, flat, and press the seam allowance towards the main fabric.

6 Fold up the hem by ⅜" (1cm) and press it.

7 Topstitch along the edge of the bias facing.

Horsehair braid hem

Above: a horsehair braid hem on the right side of a project (right), and on the wrong side (left).

If you want to add body and volume to a fabric hem, then this is the method to use. It's a vintage technique (as you might guess from the name of the braid, although it's made of synthetic materials today) and is ideal for full skirts, such as circle skirts, and dresses. The braid will show on the inside, so a lining or a crinoline might be a good idea.

Check out...

Pressing, page 30
Fell stitch, page 34
Herringbone stitch, page 35

Best used for...

Lightweight and mediumweight fabrics
Where a lining will cover the wrong side of the hem

1 Right sides together, lay one edge of the horsehair braid against the raw edge of the fabric. Position the fabric under the foot of the sewing machine so that the needle will start sewing ¼" (6mm) from the edge (a quilting foot might be useful for this). You can put in a few pins if you find it helpful, but most people find it better to guide the edges together with their hands as they sew along. Sew the braid to the fabric.

2 The cut end of the braid is stiff and can be scratchy, so at a join in the braid, slip a length of seam binding tape into the hem, positioning it so that it covers the cut end on the right side of the braid.

3 Fold up the hem to the required depth and press the fold.

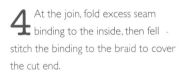

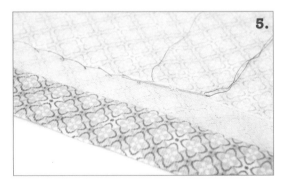

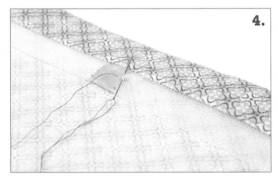

4 At the join, fold excess seam binding to the inside, then fell stitch the binding to the braid to cover the cut end.

5 Using herringbone stitch, sew the top edge of the braid to the wrong side of the fabric.

Lace-trimmed hem

Above: a lace-trimmed hem on the right side of a project (right), and on the wrong side (left).

This is a pretty hem finish for when the wrong side of the garment might show, or for a special dress. Choose lace with a robust top edge; it doesn't have to be straight, but it shouldn't be frail.

Check out...
Pressing, page 30
Slip stitch, page 34

Best used for...
All fabrics
Where the wrong side of the hem
   might show

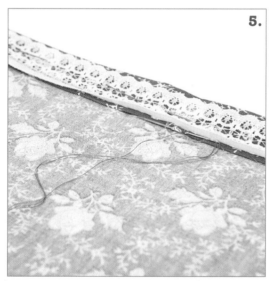

1 The hem must be deeper than the lace, so press under a double hem, then open out the second fold. Lay the top edge of the lace against the second fold and make sure it doesn't protrude beyond the edge of the first fold, as shown.

2 Fold the hem back up. Pin the lace to the hem allowance, positioning the top edge of the lace just above the fold, as shown. Do not pin right through to the main fabric.

3 Set the sewing machine to a medium straight stitch. Fold out the hem and sew the lace to the top edge of the hem allowance.

4 Fold up the hem again and pin it in place.

5 Fold back the top edge of the lace and slip stitch the hem in place behind it. The press the lace, and hem, flat.

Machine-stitched hem

If you are happy to have a line of machine stitching showing on the right side of the project, then pin the hem in Step 2 while you pin the lace in place, and sew through all layers in Step 3.

Rolled hem

This narrowest of hems isn't the easiest to sew, but it works well on very fine and sheer fabrics. The machine and hand methods are shown here, so choose the one you are most comfortable making.

Check out...
Thread tracing, page 28
Pressing, page 30
Fell stitch, page 34

Best used for...
Sheer and lightweight fabrics

By machine

The multiple lines of machining help keep the hem stable and also give it some body.

1 Trim the hem allowance accurately to ⅝" (1.5cm). Set the sewing machine to a small straight stitch and machine-sew a line ⅛" (3mm) below the intended hemline; so ½" (1.2cm) from the edge. If your machine doesn't have a throat plate marking for that distance, then use a magnetic seam guide (see page 14), or masking tape.

2 Press up the hem, pressing so that the line of machining is just rolled to the wrong side.

3 Machine-sew again, sewing exactly over the first line of stitching on the wrong side.

4 Trim the hem allowance very close to the line of stitching.

5 Fold up the hem again and press it.

6 Machine-sew a final time, sewing exactly over the visible line of stitching on the wrong side.

1.

2.

3.

4.

5.

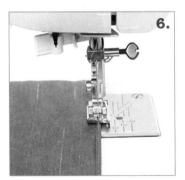
6.

Rolled hem presser foot

You can buy a presser foot that will roll a hem and stitch it all in one go; or at least, that is the theory. I have tried it several times and at some point in the hem the fabric either loosens or catches in the scroll of the foot, and everything goes awry. But if this foot works for you, then that is excellent news!

Above: a hand-rolled hem on the right side of a project (right), and on the wrong side (left).

By hand

Make sure you have scrupulously clean hands before starting this method.

1 Thread trace the hemline; you only need a small hem allowance.

2 Set the sewing machine to a small straight stitch and sew a line ⅛" (3mm) below the hemline.

3 Cut the fabric close to the stitches for 6" (15cm); don't cut more than this at a time because if the fabric frays it is harder to roll neatly.

4 Using your fingers, roll up a short length of the hem to enclose the machine stitching; the thread-traced hemline should be on the bottom edge of the roll.

5 Fell stitch the hem. Take out the thread tracing.

Machine-embroidered hem

Above: an embroidered hem on the right side of a project (right), and on the wrong side (left).

A great hem detail for some adult projects, as well as being very cute for children's items. It's always worth basting the hem before machine embroidering, and do test the stitch on a scrap of the fabric to make sure it sits within the hem turn-up, and to get the tension right.

Check out...
Pressing, page 30

Best used for...
Lightweight and mediumweight fabrics

1 It's helpful to have a fairly firm base fabric for machine embroidery, so fold up and press a double full-depth hem.

2 Baste the hem very close to the upper edge.

3 Machine-embroider along the hem. It is that simple!

Machine-embroidery with fancy threads

You can use thick or fancy threads in the bobbin and stitch the hem from the wrong side to create an effect on the right side. Turn to page 82 for instructions for doing this with free-motion embroidery, although some programmed stitches will also work well with this technique. Do experiment and practice before embarking on the project!

Hand-stitched hem

Above: a hand-stitched hem on the right side of a project (right), and on the wrong side (left).

Even the most ardent machine sewer will admit that a machined hem on a gorgeous fabric isn't the most attractive solution, and a slippery fabric can be a nightmare to machine-hem. Here is a slightly labor-intensive, but sure-fire, method for hemming a very difficult fabric, such as this stretch velvet, which is super-slippery and hates the iron.

Check out...

Basting, page 26
Thread tracing, page 28
Pressing, page 30
Herringbone stitch, page 35

Best used for...

"Difficult" fabrics

1.

2.

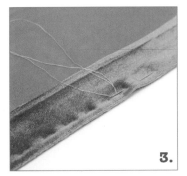

3.

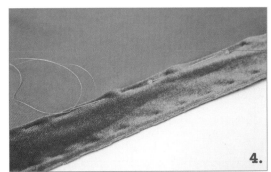

4.

1 Thread trace the hemline; this isn't necessary if the fabric presses well, which this velvet does not.

2 Press under a narrow hem along the top edge. As this will be on the wrong side, it doesn't matter if the fabric disagrees a little with the iron!

3 Fold up the hem along the thread-traced hemline and baste close to the fold.

4 Fold under the narrow hem and pin it in place. Baste close to the folded edge. The hem is completely stabilized and ready to stitch.

5 Herringbone-stitch the hem in position: this very stable stitch is better than slip stitch for tricky fabrics.

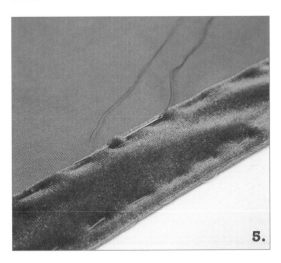

5.

Fastenings to do up

As well as being functional, a fastening can be a focal point of a project. Whether it be a purchased decorative button, a custom-made one, or a decoratively stitched zipper, there are some easy options that also look good.

Placing buttonholes

There are various "rules" as to how you should make and position buttonholes on all sorts of garments; if space allowed, I could easily devote an entire chapter to this if I went into the matter thoroughly. However, a garment pattern should give advice, and there is quite a lot of information on dressmaking sites and forums on the Web. The three main elements to be considered are spacing, size, and shape, and you should ALWAYS test your planned buttonhole on a scrap of the project fabric and slip a button through it to check that the fit is correct.

Left: rectangular and oval buttonholes can be used vertically or horizontally, with horizontal holes withstanding stress better. Keyhole buttonholes are placed horizontally and the button sits in the rounded end when fastened.

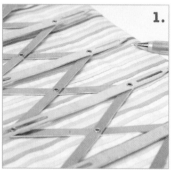

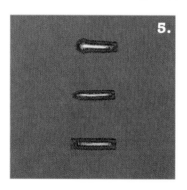

1 You can, of course, just use a ruler to measure the spacing of buttonholes, but an expanding gauge makes the process much quicker, assuming you want evenly spaced buttonholes. Concertina the gauge in and out until each long eyelet is in the perfect position for a buttonhole, then just mark the fabric through the eyelets.

2 For a flat button, just measure the width and add ⅛" (3mm) for wiggle room; this is the length you need to make your buttonhole.

3 For a button with a shank, measure the width, add the depth, and ⅛" (3mm).

4 A spherical or oddly shaped button can be measured by wrapping a strip of paper around it, creasing the paper to mark the circumference, then measuring between the creases. Half this measurement plus ⅛" (3mm) is the length the buttonhole should be.

5 There are three basic buttonhole shapes: rectangular (bottom), oval or half-oval (middle), and keyhole (top). Many sewing machines will make automatic buttonholes in these shapes (even vintage machines can often do this, using a buttonholer attachment). Rectangular and oval buttonholes are fairly similar, though the fanned stitches of an oval buttonhole will secure the threads of a loosely woven fabric better than a rectangular one will. A keyhole buttonhole is designed to accommodate the shank of a button and is best used on thick fabrics.

Hand-stitched buttonhole

There are several very good reasons for working a buttonhole by hand: they look great (with a little practice), you can use lovely, thick threads, it's easy to completely control position and size, and on delicate or slippery fabrics they can be easier to work than a machine-stitched version.

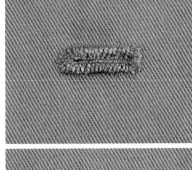

1.

2.

3.

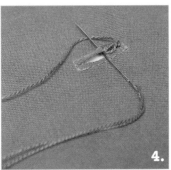
4.

5.

6.

7.

Check out...
Backstitch, page 33
Whip stitch, page 36
Buttonhole stitch, page 37
Placing buttonholes, page 62

Best used for...
All fabrics

Above: this buttonhole is worked in cotton perlé embroidery thread, although doubled sewing thread is fine, and buttonhole thread (obviously) works excellently.

1 Measure the button then mark a rectangle on the fabric; it must be the measured length plus ⅛" (3mm) wiggle room, by ¼" (6mm).

2 Making very small stitches, backstitch around the marked lines. (You can do this step on a sewing machine if you prefer.)

3 Using small, sharp scissors, carefully cut along the middle of the rectangle; do not cut the stitching.

4 Starting at one end, work buttonhole stitch along the edge of the slit. Ensure that the stitches cover the backstitching and that the knotted edge of the buttonhole stitching lies along the cut edge of the fabric.

5 At the end of the slit, fan out the stitches to work smoothly around to the other edge. This will take a bit of practice to get the stitches lying evenly, but that's where your test buttonhole(s) comes in. Buttonhole stitch along the other edge of the slit.

6 At the other end of the slit, work three straight stitches across the end of the buttonhole. These stitches should span the buttonhole stitch on either side.

7 Whip stitch over the three straight stitches to complete the buttonhole.

Covered button

You can use widely available kits to cover buttons to perfectly match your garments, or you can hunt out a specialist company to make them for you (many offer a mail-order service), which is especially useful if you need lots of buttons, or if the fabric you want to use is quite thick.

Check out...
Running stitch, page 33
Hand embroidery stitches,
    page 83

Best used for...
Lightweight and mediumweight
    fabrics

Above: a fussy-cut covered button (top) and an embroidered covered button (below).

Fussy-cut

Fussy-cutting means cutting a piece of patterned fabric in such a way as to position the motif or pattern to best advantage. For a covered button, this will usually mean centring the motif on the button.

1 A covered button kit will have a circle template—usually on the back of the packaging—that you use to cut out the piece of fabric to cover the button with. For fussy-cutting you need to make a window template, so draw around the provided template onto card or paper, then cut out and discard the drawn circle. Position the template on the fabric so that the motif you want to feature is in the right place in the window, then draw around the inside of the template.

2 Cut out the fabric circle and work a small running stitch around it, not too close to the edge.

3 Pull up the stitches around the button top, then snap on the back, following the manufacturer's instructions.

Embroidered

Not all the embroidered buttons on a project need to be the same; you could, for example, create a garden with a different flower on each of several buttons.

1 Cut a piece of fabric large enough to hold all the buttons you want to make. Lay the inner hoop on the fabric, then use the template from the button kit to draw out the required number of circles. Fit the fabric into the hoop.

2 Embroider each button, starting with a central motif if there is one. You can use a fading fabric marker to mark out the center of the button (use the snap-on back as a template) if it's helpful. Cut out the fabric circles and make up the buttons following the manufacturer's instructions.

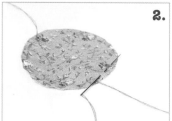

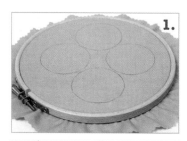

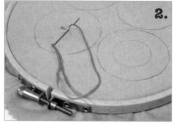

Dorset button

These traditional buttons are worked over metal (or plastic) curtain rings and have various different stitch patterns; this is an easy and popular one to get you started. The results are pretty and delicate and are lovely on lightweight, feminine garments.

1 Cut a 2yd (2m) length of stranded embroidery thread. Thread a tapestry needle, then lay the free end of the thread against the ring and start working buttonhole stitch over the ring, stitching over the free end to trap it in place. Butt the stitches right up next to each other and pull them tight. After a few stitches, cut the visible end off.

2 Continue buttonhole stitching right around the ring (this will take less time than you might think), then join the two ends of the stitching by taking the needle through the knot of the first stitch made, as shown.

3 Roll the stitching on the ring so that the row of knots faces inward. Then wind the thread right across and around the ring, as shown, to make evenly spaced spokes. This will take a bit of fiddling about to get right: you need four wraps to make eight spokes.

4 Secure the spokes by making a couple of stitches over and around them in the middle of the ring. It's important that the spokes meet right in the middle of the ring or the button will be lopsided: you can't go back and adjust the position later, so try and get it right now.

5 Start weaving the thread around the spokes: come to the front between two spokes, then take the needle over the spoke on the right, then under that spoke and under the next one to the left. Repeat, going over then under the spoke immediately to the right and under the next one to the left, until the whole wheel is filled with woven thread. Secure the thread on the center back by weaving it into the stitches. Sew the button on with matching sewing thread, making the stitches through the center of the button.

1.

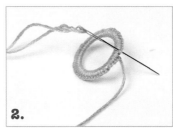
2.

3.

4.

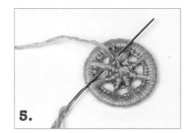
5.

Check out...
Buttonhole stitch, page 37

Best used for...
Delicate buttons

Above: this Dorset button pattern is known as a Crosswheel, or sometimes a Blandford Cartwheel.

Threads

You can make Dorset buttons using any type of fairly thick embroidery floss. Try cotton perlé—sometimes called "pearl cotton"—or coton a broder, and do experiment with multi-colored, space-dyed and variegated threads; these buttons look great worked in any of those.

Singleton button

This is another traditional button that works well on lightweight garments. Make it from the garment fabric for a perfectly co-ordinated feature, fussy-cutting it if appropriate. A metal or plastic curtain ring makes the internal frame of the button.

Above: a singleton button fussy-cut to feature a flower and leaves motif.

Check out...

Pressing, page 30
Running stitch, page 33
Backstitch, page 33
Fussy cutting, page 64

Best used for...

Lightweight and mediumweight
    fabrics
Delicate buttons

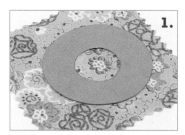

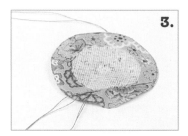

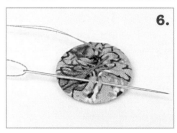

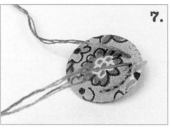

1 Draw around the curtain ring onto card, then draw a concentric circle 1" (2.5cm) larger. Cut out the template. Draw around both circles onto the fabric, using a fading fabric marker, and cut out the outer circle.

2 Cut a circle of fusible interfacing that is about ½" (1.2cm) larger than the curtain ring and iron it onto the middle of the wrong side of the fabric.

3 Work a line of small running stitches around the edge of the circle of interfacing.

4 Put the curtain ring into the middle of the fabric circle and pull up the stitches to form a pouch.

5 Use the point of a knitting needle to tuck the edges of the fabric inside the pouch, then pull up the stitches tightly. All the raw edges of the fabric should be hidden within the button, and be filling out the center a little.

6 Make several straight stitches across the back of the button to hold the fabric firmly in place.

7 Using sewing thread or three strands of six-strand floss, work a circle of backstitch just inside the ring, right around the button. Sew the button on to a project by making stitches through the gathered section on the back.

Sewing on buttons

This might seem a ridiculously simple technique to include here, but once you get beyond an ordinary shirt button, it's amazing how many people can't sew on a button properly. And, you can make the stitching a feature of plain buttons.

Check out...
Placing buttonholes, page 62

Best used for...
Two-hole buttons with no shank
Thick fabrics

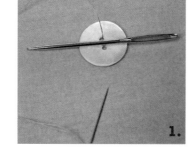

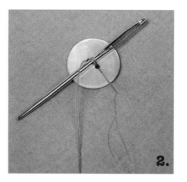

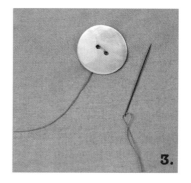

Thread shank button

Buttons that are going through buttonholes in thick fabric need to have a shank so that they lie flat on top of the buttonhole (a keyhole buttonhole is usually the best shape to use). If the button you want to use doesn't already have a metal shank, then you need to sew it on with a thread shank.

1 Bring the needle and thread up through the fabric in position, then take it through one hole in the button. Lay a thick tapestry needle or a matchstick on top of the button, between the holes.

2 Sew on the button, sewing over the tapestry needle.

3 Take the thread through a hole in the button to emerge between the button and the fabric. Slip out the tapestry needle and push the button up to the top of the thread loops. Wrap the thread around the loops five or six times, pulling it tight. Secure the thread on the back.

Above: from the top; a thread shank button; button with beads; arrow stitch pattern; cross stitch pattern; square stitch pattern.

Decoratively stitched buttons

You can make plain four-hole buttons a bit more interesting by sewing them on with different stitch patterns: you can stitch a cross, a square, or an arrow.
To add beads to a button, sew it on in the usual way. Then—using a beading needle if necessary—repeat the stitches, threading on enough beads to span the gaps between the holes.

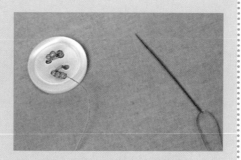

Hand-picked zipper

If you have always struggled to insert zippers, especially invisible ones, this is a solution you might like. It has a lovely vintage look to it, and indeed is still the way many couture and vintage sewers prefer to install a zipper.

Check out...
Basting, page 26
Pressing, page 30
Pick stitch, page 33
Beading, page 78

Best used for...
All fabrics

1 Before sewing the seam you need to stabilize the zipper seam allowances: this really will make the sewing easier and the end result will both look better and be stronger. Cut strips of lightweight fusible interfacing that are just a tiny bit narrower than the seam allowances. Fuse them to the wrong side of the fabric, along the edges of the zipper section. Sew up the seam below the zipper, then press the seam allowances open, including the open, stabilized, zipper sections.

2 Open the zipper and lay one side of it under the appropriate seam allowance, positioning the pressed edge of the fabric so that it just covers the zipper teeth. Pin and then baste this side in place through the zipper tape.

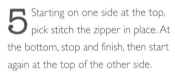

5 Starting on one side at the top, pick stitch the zipper in place. At the bottom, stop and finish, then start again at the top of the other side.

6 You can add beads to the pick stitching to embellish a zipper, just thread one onto every stitch. Cut a strip of card to use as a spacer to create a neat, even line of beads.

Above: one side of this zipper is simply pick-stitched, the other is embellished with beads.

3 Close the zipper and pin the lower end of the other side in place to the other seam allowance.

4 Open the zipper again and pin then baste the rest of the other side in place, positioning the fold of the fabric as before. Do the zipper up to check that you are happy with the way the fabric meets over it (see right).

Zipper fit

If the garment is tight fitting then remember that when it's worn the fabric will pull apart a tiny amount at the zipper, so the edges should push against one another, creating a tiny ridge over the zipper when relaxed.

Exposed zipper

This has been a recent trend in fashion design, and it is an easy way of putting in a zipper. You can make even more of a feature of the zipper by embellishing it with embroidery stitches—hand or machine stitches—or beading.

Check out...
Basting, page 26
Pressing, page 30
Topstitched seam, page 43
Hand embroidery stitches,
  page 83

Best used for...
All fabrics

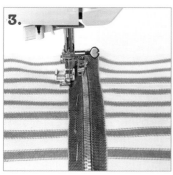
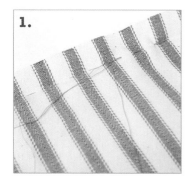
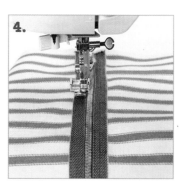

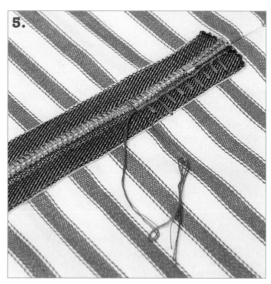

1 Sew the seam below the zipper. Baste along the seam line of the zipper section to close it, then press the seam allowances open.

2 Lay the zipper in place on the right side of the seam, making sure that the teeth are exactly over the basted opening. Pin the zipper in place. If you prefer, you can baste it before machine stitching.

3 Set the sewing machine to a medium straight stitch and fit a zipper foot. Topstitch along the outer edges of the zipper tape, very close to the edge. Start stitching at the same end on each tape.

4 Topstitch very close to the zipper teeth, again starting at the same end each time. Remove the basting.

5 If you want to, you can embellish the zipper tapes; here, they are embroidered with irregular blanket stitching in perlé floss.

Above: one side of this exposed zipper is embellished with stitching, the other side is left plain.

Snaps

Sometimes called press studs, these are a discreet way of fastening two pieces of fabric; though only if fabric is not very thick, and the join is not going to be under strain. Snaps aren't that strong and can burst apart unexpectedly.

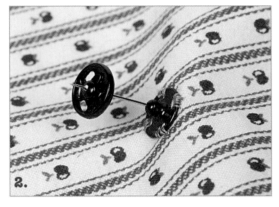

Best used for

Lightweight and mediumweight fabrics

1 Sew on the protruding half of the snap first, sewing four or five small, neat oversewing stitches through each hole.

2 To position the other half of the snap, first slip a needle up through the hole in the middle of the sewn-on half. Slip the hole in the other half onto the needle.

3 Push the needle into the fabric where you want the other half of the snap to be. Slip the half stud down the needle so that it sits in the right position. Holding it in place, sew it on as for the first half.

Choosing metal fastenings

Snaps usually come in either silver or black and are functional rather than attractive. However, you can buy colored metal versions, and in a large size these can be a feature on a garment as well as a closure. Metal hooks and eyes—or skirt hooks—are very rarely found in anything other than silver, gold, or black, but you can buy fur hooks, which are large hook and eye fastenings that are covered in wrapped cord or gimp. These are commonly available in white, cream, and black, and specialist notions stores sometimes have them in other colors, too. They are a bit too chunky for lighter garments, but good for coats—fur ones or wool ones.

Hook and eye

These fastenings will happily take a lot more strain than snaps, and are equally discreet, although not quite as flat. However, you can get flat hooks and eyes, which are also known as skirt hooks or trouser hooks.

Check out...
Buttonhole stitch, page 37

Best used for
All fabrics

1 Sew on the hook half first. Start by sewing a few straight stitches over the straight, flat part of the hook to hold it in position, and to help it lie flat when closed.

2 Sew around each eye: you can use oversewing stitches as with a snap (see opposite), but it does look neater—and is a little more stable—to use buttonhole stitches. Sew on the eye in the same way.

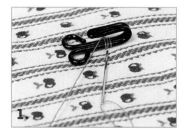

Thread loop

A loop made of thread that matches the fashion fabric is a couture-style touch that works especially well on delicate fabrics, if the fastening is not going to be under strain. A flat loop like this one will replace a metal eye (see above), while a protruding loop can be used instead of a buttonhole.

Check out...
Buttonhole stitch, page 37

Best used for
Lightweight fabrics

1 Using single sewing thread, make three or four straight stitches the size and position of the loop.

2 Starting at one end of the straight stitches, work buttonhole stitches over the threads, not catching the fabric at any point. Use the tip of the needle to nudge the buttonhole stitches up against one another, and continue until the whole loop is covered with tightly packed buttonhole stitches. At the other end of the loop, take the thread through to the back and secure it.

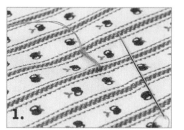

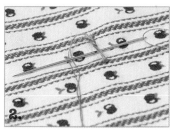

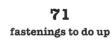

Above: from the top; snap; hook and eye sewn on with buttonhole stitch; skirt hook and eye sewn on with oversewing stitches, thread loop for a hook.

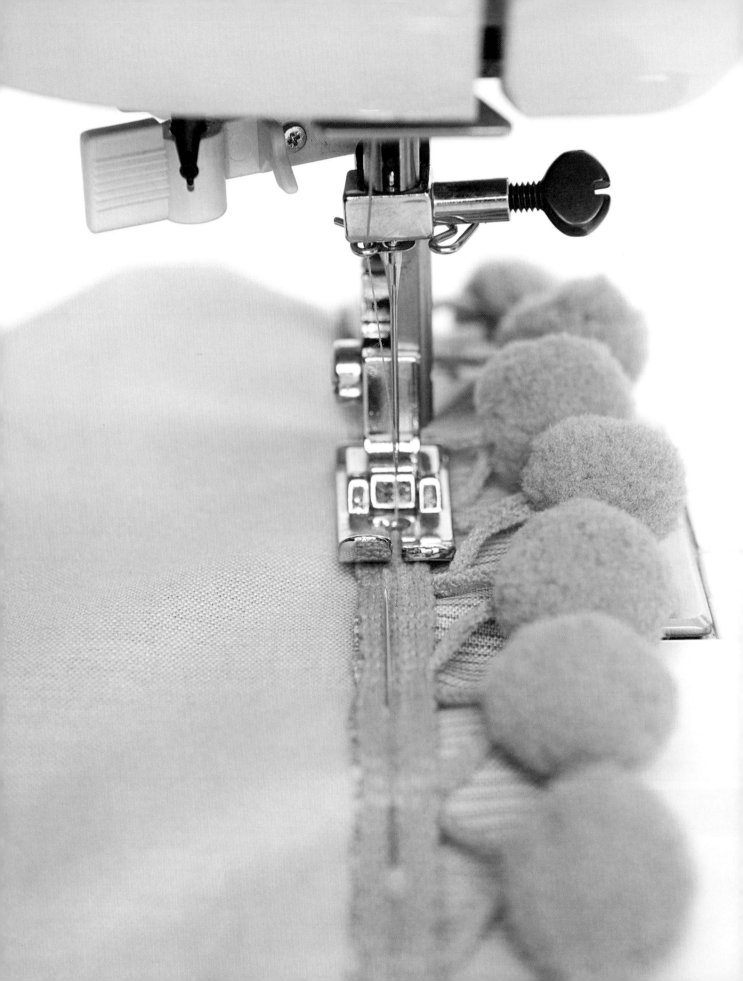

Embellishments to add

There are myriad elements you can add to stitched projects to detail and highlight areas, refine color schemes, add texture, stamp personality, and generally customize even the plainest pattern. This chapter looks at some of the options you might choose.

Trims

Detailing attachment methods for every type of trim available would require several books, and they would be outdated as soon as they reached the bookshelves because new and gorgeous products appear all the time. However, there are some general principles you can follow that should stand you in good stead with lots of different trims.

Marabou

This method of hand-stitching trims can be applied to cords and braids, as well as more exotic trims such as this marabou feather. The stitch is similar to fell stitch.

Check out...
Fell stitch, page 34

Best used for...
Trims with a solid core/top edge, such as braids and cords

Above: marabou feather trim.

Left: embroidered flower trim.

1.

2.

3.

1 Use a fading fabric marker to mark the position of the trim on the fabric. Thread a needle with sewing thread that matches the trim, knot the end, and bring it up through the fabric where you want the trim to start.

2 Take a tiny straight stitch through the trim. If the trim has a distinctly wrong side, then stitch into that, ensuring that the stitch doesn't show on the right side. Here, the feathers are pushed apart as much as possible to avoid catching them in the stitch.

3 Make a short stitch through the fabric, and pull the thread taut. Repeat Steps 2 and 3 along the trim.

Embroidered trim

This method can be used with any embroidered trim or patch and if the thread is matched carefully, the stitches will be completely invisible.

Check out...
Pick stitch, page 33

Best used for...
Embroidered trims and patches

Using sewing thread that matches the trim, simply make tiny pick stitches into the embroidered sections, being very careful to follow the direction of the existing stitches. Work as close to the edge as possible, and put at least one stitch into each shaped area (such as each petal in this trim).

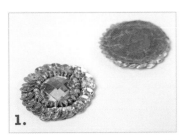

Backed trims

This is an invisible method of sewing on trims and motifs that have a fabric backing.

1 Beaded and sequined trims are often worked onto a thin fabric. The first step is to cut off any loose threads or areas of fabric that show from the front, though be careful not to cut the stitches holding the trim together.

2 Using sewing thread that matches the backing fabric (for clarity, contrast thread is used here), bring the needle up through the fabric at the position of the edge of the trim. Put the trim in place, then make a slanting stitch under the edge but through the fabric backing and into the main fabric. Repeat to sew the trim in position around (or along) the edge. Make the stitches as deep into the backing fabric as possible to prevent them pulling out.

3 Also sew close to the center (or along a lower edge), making tiny pick stitches up through the trim and back down into the main fabric.

Check out...

Pick stitch, page 33

Best used for...

Backed trims and motifs

Below: sequin trim.

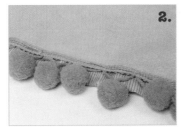

Edge trims

Some fringes and bobble trims have attractive bands along the top edge, but many do not and the trim looks better if the band is concealed. This method allows you to do that, and to turn up a hem at the same time.

Check out...

Topstitched seam, page 43

Best used for...

Edge trims with an unattractive top edge

1 Right sides together, pin the solid top edge of the trim to the edge of the fabric, so that the decorative part of the trim is lying on the fabric, as shown. Thread the sewing machine with thread that matches the main fabric, set it to a medium straight stitch, and sew the trim in place. (The raw edge can be serged before sewing on the trim, if required.)

2 Turn up the hem the required amount: here, just the bobbles will peek out on the right side.

3 Once you are happy with the position of the trim, sew the hem in place, sewing over the first line of stitches.

Right: pom-pom trim.

Piping

You can make piping with a zipper foot, but using a specially designed piping foot does make the whole process quicker and easier, and you get perfect piping every time. Dealing with curves and corners and joining ends are not difficult techniques to get right.

Check out...
Pressing, page 30

Best used for...
Lightweight and mediumweight fabrics

Making piping

A piping foot removes any need for basting, and you only need to pin if the fabric is tricky to handle—for example, satin or velvet.

1.

1 Cut a bias strip that measures double the width of the piping cord plus double the required seam allowance, by the length required. At one end, fold the strip over the cord, matching the raw edges of the fabric, and pin it in place. When using a piping foot there is no need to pin the rest of the strip if the fabric isn't slippery.

2 Fit the piping foot and set the sewing machine to a medium straight stitch. Put the piping under the foot so that the cord sits in one of the channels, and start to sew. Keep the raw edges of the fabric aligned as the piping feeds through the machine.

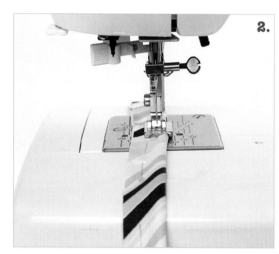
2.

3 To attach the piping to a straight edge, pin the raw edge of the piping right sides together to the raw edge of the fabric. Sew with the piping foot as before, sewing over the previous line of stitching. If the fabrics are stable, you can skip Step 2 and make the piping and sew it to the fabric at the same time, though it's worth pinning it all in place first if you do that.

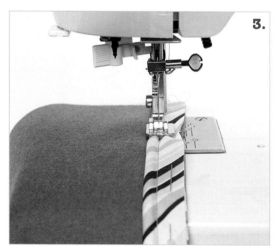
3.

Patterns on the bias

Fabric patterns such as stripes and checks can look really interesting cut on the bias. Try piping a stripe project in the main fabric; the contrast between the straight-grain stripes of the flat sections and the slanting stripes on the bias-cut piping can be very effective. The same applies to checkered patterns, especially those with quite small check squares, such as gingham.

Joining piping

Try to join piping on a straight edge as it'll be easier to deal with the ends. The length of piping needs to be 1" (2.5cm) longer than the edge it'll be sewn to.

1 Start sewing on the piping ⅝" (1.5cm) from one end.

2 Sew on the piping until you get to ⅜" (1cm) from the starting point, then reverse to secure the stitching. At this finishing end, unpick the stitching holding the fabric around the cord.

3 Trim the piping cord to butt up to the starting end. Fold under ⅝" (1.5cm) of the free fabric.

4 Slip the folded end of fabric over the loose starting end. Adjust the cord and fabric until it all lies neatly, then topstitch across the join, matching the existing stitching line.

Piping corners and curves

Clipping the seam allowances of the piping will help you to negotiate corners neatly and curves smoothly.

1 For a corner, pin the piping to the fabric up to the corner. On the next edge, measure in the depth of the seam allowance and put in a pin to mark it, as shown.

2 In line with the marking pin, clip the piping seam allowance almost up to the stitching.

3 Bend the piping round the corner, and pin the next edge in place.

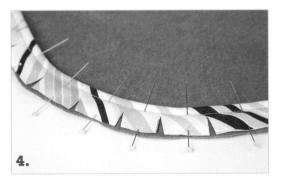

4 For a curve, clip the seam allowance at regular intervals as you bend and pin it in place. Tighter curves will need more frequent clips.

Above a smoothly piped edge is easy to achieve with a piping foot.

Beading

Beads offer a lovely way of adding detail and sparkle to a project. There are hundreds of colors available in a range of sizes and finishes, so there's bound to be something to suit your project. Don't bead very lightweight fabrics because the fibers can be too frail or loosely woven to support many beads.

Check out...
Backstitch, page 33
Pick stitch, page 33

Best used for...
Thick and mediumweight
fabrics

Above: a few single beads run into a couched line of beads, that runs into a strand of fringe.

Single bead

Sewing on a single bead is easy: use a beading needle and strong beading thread.

Bring the needle up through the fabric at the position of the bead. Thread on the bead, then take the needle back down a bead's length away from where it came out. Secure the thread on the back with a couple of tiny backstitches just through a few of threads of the fabric, directly under the bead where it won't show. If you are adding a number of single beads close together, then sew them on with pick stitch, one bead threaded on for each stitch.

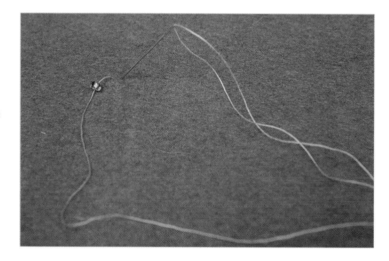

Types of beads

Seed beads are the most commonly available type: they are more or less circular with slightly flattened tops and bases, where the hole is. Bugle beads are the long thin tubes, and delica beads are the very short tubes; indeed, the latter are sometimes called cylinder beads. Hex or 2-cut beads have faceted flat sides, while fire-polished beads are faceted round beads. Most types come in a variety of sizes.

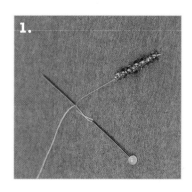

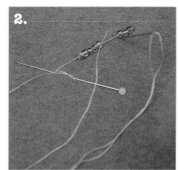

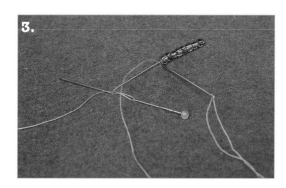

Couched beads

You need a beading needle threaded with beading thread and a sewing needle threaded with sewing thread to work a line of beads using this method.

Flawed beads

Before stringing a lot of beads onto thread, do check them for misshapen or otherwise flawed beads. If you have threaded on a misshapen bead, followed by a lot of other beads, you can try crushing it off the thread with pliers. Wear safety glasses when doing this to protect your eyes.

1 Bring the beading needle and thread up through the fabric at the start of the line. Thread on a few beads; ten is plenty to start with. Lay the string of beads along the line you want them to follow, put a pin in the fabric on that line and wind the thread around it to hold the beads tautly on the line.

2 Slide some beads up the thread until there are only three at the start of the line. Bring the sewing needle and thread up through the fabric, on the line and right next to the third bead. Make a stitch over the beading thread, going down where the needle came out. Pull the sewing thread taut.

3 Slide three more beads along the thread to sit next to the first three and repeat Step 2. Thread on more beads and continue in this way.

Beaded fringe

Fringes can be simple, or elaborate, long or short; either way they add movement and texture to any project.

1 If required, mark the positions of the fringe strands on the fabric with a fading fabric marker. Bring a beading needle and strong beading thread out through the edge of the fabric. Thread on the bead sequence for a single strand of fringe, ending with a small round bead.

2 Skipping the last bead, take the needle back up through the rest of them and through the edge of the fabric. Secure the strand on the back as for a single bead (see opposite): that way if you catch a strand of fringe and it breaks, only that strand's beads will be lost.

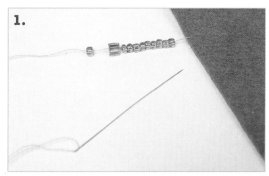

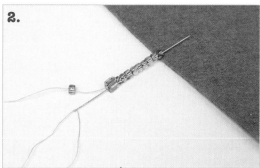

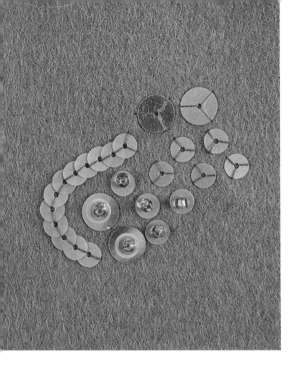

Above: sequins sewn on using all three methods. To the right of the line of sequins are stacks of sequins under a bead, made by just threading on the required arrangement before adding the bead.

Sequins

Sequins are another lovely, shimmery embellishment that's easy to apply. Do remember that you cannot really press anything with sequins as they will just shrivel up from the heat of the iron. A very quick press with a cool iron on the back of the fabric can be risked, but I would test a swatch first. Use beading or sewing thread for sequins.

Check out...

Pressing, page 30
Beading, page 78

Best used for...

All fabrics

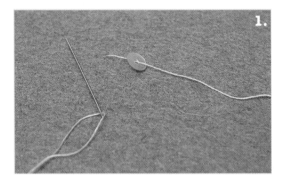

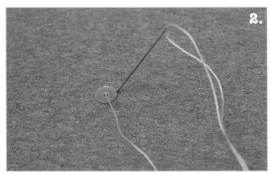

Single sequin

This is the best way to sew on a single sequin using stitches; it's sometimes called "star-stitching a sequin."

1 Bring the needle and thread up through the fabric at the position of the sequin. Thread on a sequin.

2 Take the needle back down through the fabric, right at the edge of the sequin.

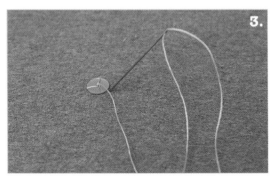

3 Bring the needle up through the hole in the sequin and make two more stitches, spacing them evenly, like a simple star.

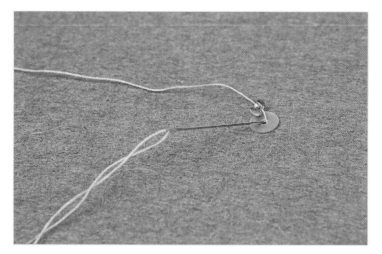

Single sequin with bead

Here, you are using a bead to hold the sequin in place, so the bead must be larger than the hole in the sequin.

Bring the needle and thread up through the fabric at the position of the sequin. Thread on a sequin and then a bead. Skipping the bead, take the needle back down through the sequin and fabric. Secure the thread on the back as for a single bead.

Line of sequins

This method produces a line of overlapping sequins.

1 Bring the needle and thread up through the fabric at the position of the sequin. Thread on a sequin and take the needle back down through the fabric, right at the edge of the sequin. Bring it up again on the opposite edge of the sequin, as shown.

2 Thread on a second sequin. Take the needle down through the hole in the first sequin.

3 Bring the needle up on the far edge of the last sequin stitched down, thread on another, then take the needle down through the hole in the last sequin stitched down. Repeat to produce a line of sequins.

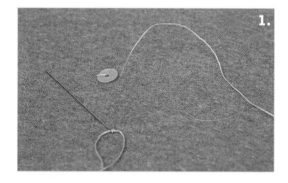

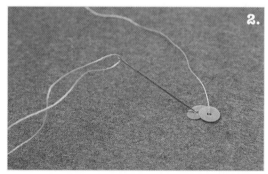

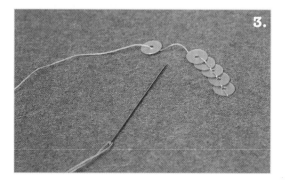

Types of sequins

There are two main types of circular sequin, flat—as used here—and cupped. The cupped ones are shaped like a shallow dish with faceted sides, and these facets catch the light and make the sequin twinkle more than a flat sequin will. There are also shaped sequins, available in a huge range of designs and colors, such as the snowflake sequins used on the Christmas Decoration project on page 106.

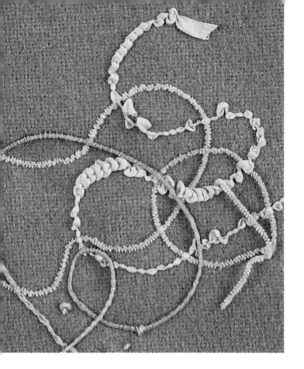

Machine embroidery bobbin work

One restriction of machine embroidery is that the thread needs to fit through the eye of the needle; but it doesn't if you put the thick thread on the bobbin and sew upside down. As you can't see exactly what you are doing, this does take a bit of practice, but once you've got all the tensions right, it's a very creative way to embroider.

Left: the palest line is made with silk ribbon on the bobbin, the middle color is a chenille thread, and the darkest a knitting yarn.

Best used for...

Thick and mediumweight fabrics

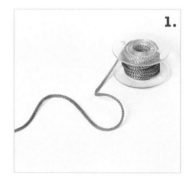

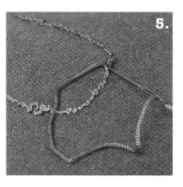

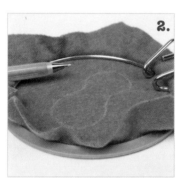

1 Wind the thick thread onto the bobbin. If it's on a spool then you might be able to do this on the machine; if not then hand-wind it keeping a gentle, even tension.

2 As you are working on the back of the fabric, you can draw on the shape you want to embroider. Fasten the fabric in a hoop.

3 Fit an embroidery foot and drop the feed dogs on the sewing machine. Thread the top spool with ordinary sewing thread and load the specially wound bobbin into the case. Put the hoop under the needle and start sewing: all you will see is the ordinary top thread.

4 When you have finished sewing, turn the fabric over to see how the thick thread has responded to stitching; the results can sometimes be surprising.

5 To take the ends of thick threads through to the back, just thread them into a tapestry needle and push that through the fabric.

Hand embroidery stitches

There are many styles of hand embroidery—some with traditions stretching back centuries—and many hundreds of individual stitches to explore, which we don't have space to cover here. If you do take to hand embroidery, then you will end up with favorite stitches; these are some of mine.

Check out...

Hand utility stitches, page 33

Best used for...

All fabrics

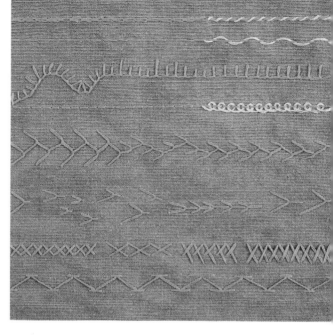

Above: from the top; chain stitch, whipped on the right; running stitch, laced on the right; blanket stitch, which can be worked around curves and corners by angling the "leg" stitches, and can have different-length "legs"; backstitch, laced on the right to become Pekinese Stitch; feather stitch in various different sizes, and in the middle it's worked with two stitches running in each direction to become double feather stitch; fly stitch, worked singly with different-shaped Vs and different length legs, and worked in a line; cross stitch, worked in different sizes and, second from right, with different-length "arms"; chevron stitch worked with different-length straight stitches.

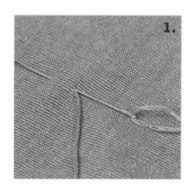

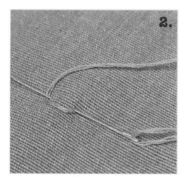

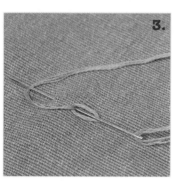

Chain stitch

This is a great stitch, and very forgiving if you are an embroidery novice.

1 Bring the needle up through the fabric at the start of the line of stitching. Take it back down next to where it came out and make a small, straight stitch: do not pull the needle through.

2 Wrap the working thread under the tip of the needle, then pull the needle through to form a loop.

3 Take the needle back down next to where it last came out and make another stitch, the same length as the first one. Wrap the thread under the needle and pull through. Repeat this step to make a linked line of stitches. Anchor the last stitch with a small straight stitch over the end of the loop.

Cross stitch

This is probably the most popular embroidery stitch in the world, and is always charming. The top stitch should always slope in the same direction within a cross stitch embroidery.

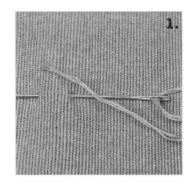

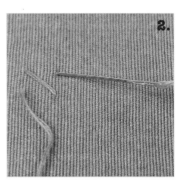

1 Bring the needle up through the fabric at top left of the first stitch. Make a short diagonal stitch to the bottom right into the fabric, then bring the needle out to the left, in line with where it went in, and below where it came out.

2 Pull the thread through, then make a second diagonal stitch to the top right to complete one cross stitch.

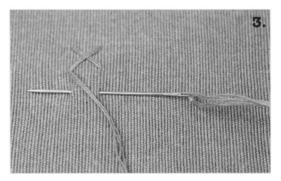

3 Bring the needle out bottom left, where the second diagonal stitch started, and you are ready to work the next cross stitch.

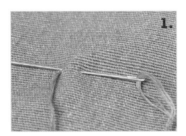

Chevron stitch

This stitch might seem a little complex, but once you get the hang of it, it grows satisfyingly quickly. It involves short straight stitches and longer diagonal ones, and, slightly counter-intuitively, it's worked from left to right.

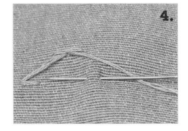

1 Bring the needle up through the fabric at the bottom left of the line of stitching. Take a short stitch straight to the right, bringing the needle out where it went in.

2 Make a longer diagonal stitch into the fabric up and to the right, bringing the needle out in a straight line a short distance to the left, as shown.

3 Make a straight stitch into the fabric to the right, bringing the needle out again at the top of the diagonal stitch.

4 Make a longer diagonal stitch into the fabric down and to the right, bringing the needle out in a straight line a short distance to the left, as shown.

5 Repeat Step 3, bringing the needle out at the bottom of the diagonal stitch. Repeat Steps 2-5 to work the stitch.

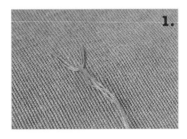

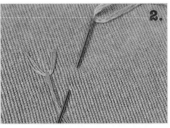

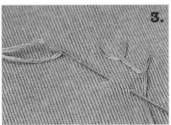

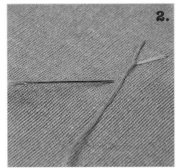

Feather stitch

If you want to make very regular feather stitch, it's helpful to draw in some guidelines to mark the width of the stitches. However, feather stitch is one of those stitches that looks lovely worked irregularly, so try it both ways.

1 Bring the needle up through the fabric at the top left of the line of stitching. Make a straight stitch into the fabric directly to the right, bringing the needle out below and midway between where it came out and where it went in, as for fly stitch (see below). Pull the thread through.

2 Make a straight stitch into the fabric immediately to the right, bringing the needle out below and midway between where it came out and where it went in, as shown.

3 Repeat Step 2, but working to the left this time. Continue in this way, making stitches to the right and left alternately.

Other stitches

Some of the hand utility stitches (see page 33) can also be used decoratively. Running stitch, backstitch, and herringbone stitch are all embroidery classics. Work buttonhole stitch with the "legs" spaced apart and you have the ever-popular blanket stitch.

Fly stitch

A versatile stitch that can be worked singly or linked together to make a line. You can alter the length of the straight stitch, and place it centrally or off-set it.

1 Bring the needle up through the fabric at the top left of the stitch. Make a straight stitch into the fabric directly to the right, bringing the needle out below and midway between where it came out and where it went in.

2 Make a straight stitch to anchor the V-shaped stitch. That's one fly stitch completed.

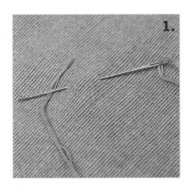

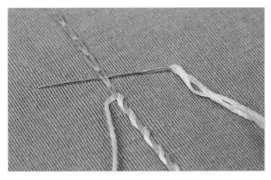

Whipped stitches

You can change the look of a stitch, and add extra color, very easily by either whipping or lacing it. The principle is the same, but when you whip a stitch you insert the needle from the same side each time, and when you lace it you insert the needle from alternate sides (see sample, page 83).

All sorts of stitches can be whipped or laced. Whipped chain stitch looses its loopy look and gains a colorful barbershop twist.

Piping, pleating, patchwork...

It's really easy to turn flat fabric into a three-dimensional element that can add detail or be a focal point of a project. There are many options—pleats, folds, gathers, stitching...and much more—but here are some of my favorite fabric manipulation techniques, which also work well in practical projects.

Yo-yos

Traditionally, these little gathered circles of fabric (also called Suffolk puffs) were sewn together to make quilt tops and pillow shams, and offered—as they still do—a decorative way of using up choice bits of fabric from the scrap bag. It doesn't take much to give them a contemporary twist.

Check out...
Running stitches, page 33

Best used for...
Lightweight and mediumweight fabrics

Simple yo-yo

Above: be aware that the wrong side of the fabric will show in the middle of a simple yo-yo.

Below: A contrast lining enlivens a plain yo-yo, and will hide the wrong side of the fabric if that is unattractive.

This is the most basic type of yo-yo.

1 Cut a circle of fabric twice the diameter you want the finished yo-yo to be (use compasses or draw around a plate). Using your fingers, press under a very narrow hem around part of the edge of the circle.

2 Thread a sewing needle with sewing thread, double it and knot the ends. Starting on the wrong side, work a line of small running stitches along the folded hem.

3 Continue right around the circle, finger-pressing under the hem as you go. End with the needle coming out on the right side. Pull up the stitches as tightly as possible.

4 Take the needle through to the wrong side and secure it with a few overstitches through the hem. Flatten the puff and arrange it so that the gathered hole is in the center.

Contrast-lined yo-yo

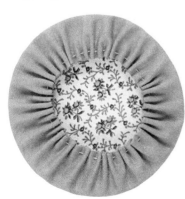

This yo-yo has a contrast center. The lining and fusible webbing also make it flatter and stiffer than a simple yo-yo.

1 Cut a circle twice the diameter of the required finished yo-yo, less ⅜" (1cm). Following the manufacturer's instructions, iron fusible webbing onto the back of a piece of contrast fabric, then draw a circle on this that is the required size of the finished yo-yo. Cut the circle out and iron it into the center of the large circle.

2 Follow Steps 2–4 of Simple Yo-Yo to complete this version, but don't pull the gathers up tight, just pull until the yo-yo is the required size, so that you can see plenty of the contrast lining.

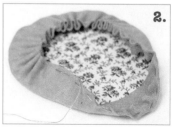

Sewn-down yo-yo

These yo-yos work really well as embellishments on all sorts of projects, and can be worked off-center for a quirky look (see page 102).

1 Cut a circle twice the diameter of the required finished yo-yo, less ⅜" (1cm). On the wrong side, use a fabric marker and compasses to draw a central circle the size of the finished yo-yo.

2 Pin the fabric circle to the backing fabric in the required position, making sure the pin is within the drawn circle. Set the sewing machine to a small straight stitch. Sewing slowly and carefully, sew right around the drawn circle.

3 Follow Steps 2–4 of Simple Yo-Yo to complete this version, but don't pull up the gathers too tight or the yo-yo won't lie flat..

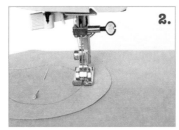

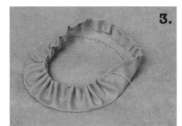

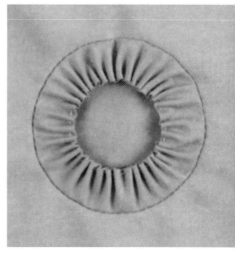

Above: sewn-down yo-yos look as though they grow out of matching background fabric.

Choosing fabrics

Lightweight and mediumweight cotton and linen fabrics make the best yo-yos. Fabrics that are very floppy don't work well as they don't have enough body to create a proper disc shape. Some silk, such as dupioni silk, is stiff enough, but it can fray so quickly and horribly that it can be tricky to make small yo-yos neatly—reserve it for larger projects. Lightweight wool fabric, the kind sold for summer-weight men's suits, also works surprisingly well on larger yo-yos. I have made a yo-yo from thin craft felt, but it was a bit lumpy, and likewise a chenille fabric made a rather chunky yo-yo.

Contrast-lined sewn-down yo-yo

This is a combination of two of the previous yo-yos. Cut a circle of main fabric and a circle of webbing-backed contrast fabric as for a Contrast-Lined Yo-Yo. Iron the contrast circle onto the main fabric, then sew the yo-yo to the backing fabric as for a Sewn-Down Yo-Yo, sewing around the edge of the contrast circle. Follow Steps 2–4 of Simple Yo-Yo to complete this version, but only pull the gathers up until the yo-yo is the required size, so that you can see the contrast lining.

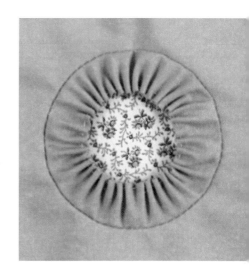

Above: fill the center of a sewn-down yo-yo with a circle of a contrast fabric.

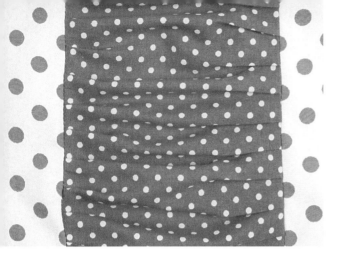

Inset ruffle

You can pleat or gather the inset strip by hand, but a ruffler foot does produce beautifully neat and even pleats that work brilliantly inset between flat fabric strips. Use this technique to create feature panels on garments, bags, quilts…whatever looks good to you.

Above: the ruffle strip can be made from the main fashion fabric, or a contrast, as here.

Check out...

Pressing, page 30

Best used for...

Lightweight and mediumweight fabrics

1 Follow the ruffler foot instructions to set the pleat depth and spacing you want; here it is medium depth and every six stitches (experimenting on a scrap of the project fabric is always a good idea). Ruffle one edge of a strip of fabric.

2 Starting from the opposite end to the first edge, ruffle the other edge. The pleats will face in opposite directions on each edge, and this is what makes the inset strip so dimensional.

3 Pin a ruffled edge right sides together with a flat piece of fabric, having the ruffled piece uppermost. Set the sewing machine to a medium straight stitch and sew the pieces together, stitching fractionally inside the line of ruffle stitching. Repeat on the opposite edge.

4 Trim the seam allowances to ⅜" (1cm).

5 Press the very edge of the ruffled strip, pressing the seam allowances towards it, and being careful not to crush the ruffles.

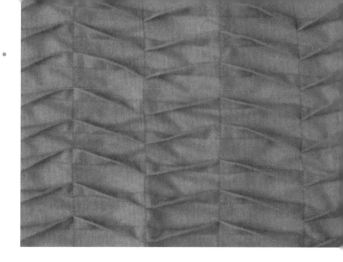

Stitched-down tucks

Just a few of these tucks can be used as a feature in a project, or a whole piece can be tucked and stitched, thought this does result in quite a stiff fabric, maybe best used for items such as bags.

Check out...

Pressing, page 30

Best used for...

Lightweight and mediumweight fabrics

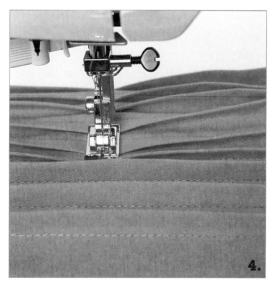

Above: the rippling tucks catch the light effectively, making the surface very animated.

1 Fold and press the fabric along the line of the first tuck.

2 Measure along to were you want the second tuck, and fold and press the fabric again. The tucks can be as tightly spaced as you want, or even irregularly spaced.

3 Starting with the first pressed line, fold the fabric and position it in the machine at the required tuck depth; here, the tucks are ⅜" (1cm) deep. Sew each tuck in turn.

4 Once all the tucks are stitched, turn the fabric and put it in the machine so that the tucks are running side-to-side. Sew across them, making sure that each one lies in the same direction as you sew over it.

5 Starting at the opposite edge of the fabric, sew across the tucks again. Make sure that the tucks all lie in the opposite direction to the way they did in the first row of stitching. You can use a quilt guide to keep the lines of stitching evenly spaced.

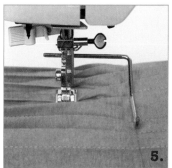

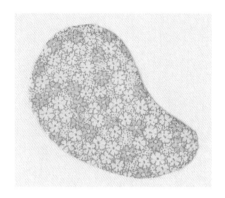

Above: left to right; a turned edge, a corded edge, and a machined edge.

Appliqué

There are three appliqué methods shown here, and the one you choose will depend in part on whether you prefer hand or machine sewing. Also, the methods offer a very different finished look, so do consider your project as a whole before picking which technique to use.

Check out...
Pressing, page 30
Fell stitch, page 34

Best used for...
Lightweight and mediumweight fabrics

Turned edge

This is the most traditional method of appliqué and is entirely hand-stitched.

1 Using a fading fabric marker, draw the shape you want onto the wrong side of the fabric. Cut it out ¼" (6mm) outside the drawn line.

2 Pin the shape to the background fabric.

3 Finger-press under a ¼" (6mm) hem on a small section of one edge. Thread a sewing needle with sewing thread and bring it up through the background fabric and through the folded edge of the appliqué piece.

4 Fell stitch the shape to the background, turning under the edge as you go.

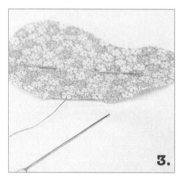
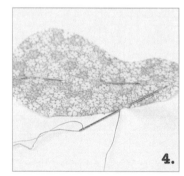

Turning the edge

You can turn under the edge as you sew, as shown here, or turn under and baste the edge of the shape, then sew it to the fabric, then remove the basting thread. The method you choose will depend on your skill and the complexity of the shape. You can clip the seam allowances on tight curves in the same way as for shaped seams (see page 41).

Corded edge

This decorative edging can be used on a bonded edge, as here, or on a hand-sewn edge (see opposite). You can use a fancy embroidery floss or knitting yarn, or a traditional cord for the edging.

1 Iron a piece of fusible webbing onto the wrong side of the fabric and draw the shape you want to appliqué on the paper backing.

2 Cut out the shape, peel off the backing, and iron the shape onto the background fabric.

3 Thread a sewing needle with sewing thread and bring it up through the background fabric, just outside the edge of the shape.

4 Lay the cord along the edge of the shape, leaving a free 2" (5cm) tail. Take the needle over the cord and into the fabric just inside the edge of the shape. Pull the stitch tight.

5 Continue in this way to sew the cord around the edge of the shape. Always bring the needle up just outside the shape and take it down just inside. To finish, thread the ends of cord into a tapestry needle and take them through to the wrong side. Secure them with a few whip stitches using sewing thread.

1.

2.

3.

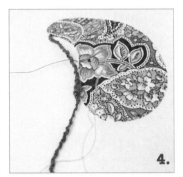

4.

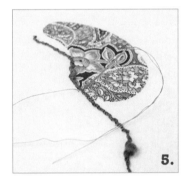

5.

Machined edge

This is quite a quick option, but you do need to practice to make the satin stitching smooth and even.

Follow Steps 1 and 2 of corded edge to attach the shape to the background. Set the sewing machine to a tight zigzag, and sew around the edge of the shape. If you stop stitching midway to adjust the direction of the material under the presser foot, do so with the needle down on the outer edge of the shape to keep the outline as smooth as possible.

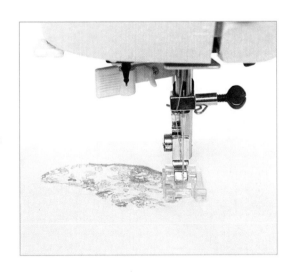

Hexagon patchwork

Sometimes called "English patchwork," this is a traditional technique that revolves around seven-patch blocks that tessellate together. Although the patch preparation and hand-sewing take time, the work is very portable (work on your lap in front of the television), and can be set aside and returned to as the mood takes you.

Check out...
Basting, page 26
Pressing, page 30
Whip stitch, page 36

Best used for...
Lightweight and mediumweight fabrics

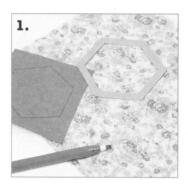

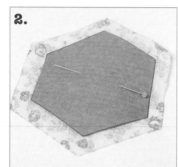

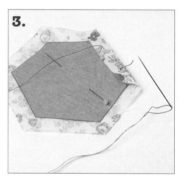

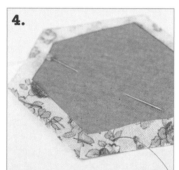

1 You will need hexagon templates for this patchwork technique: use those printed in the back of this book (see page 126), or buy commercial plastic templates, as shown here. Draw around the smaller template onto paper and the larger one onto fabric. Cut out these hexagons accurately: the success of your patchwork depends a lot on these shapes being precise.

2 Pin a paper hexagon to the wrong side of one of the fabric pieces, centering it as precisely as you can.

3 Fold one edge of the fabric over the paper and press it firmly with your fingers. You need to be accurate with all the folding and finger pressing so that your hexagons are all the same size. Starting on the back, baste through the fabric and paper along the folded edge, bringing the needle through to the back again.

4 Fold over the adjacent edge of the fabric and finger-press it, making sure that the corner is neat and sharp. Do not pull the fabric too tight or you will distort the shape of the patch. Baste along that folded edge. Continue in this way right around the hexagon, folding over and basting each edge in turn. Secure the end of the thread with a couple of backstitches through the first folded edge, stitching through the fabric only. Remove the pin. Prepare seven hexagon patches in this way, and choose one to be the center patch of the block.

5 Hold the center patch and one other (patch two) right sides together, matching the edges. Using tiny whip stitches, sew the patches together along one edge. The stitches should go through just the very edge of the fabric, not through the paper.

6 Secure the thread with three or four stitches through the folded edge and cut it.

7.

8.

9.

10.

Above: a seven-patch hexagon patchwork block in a pink palette.

7 Hold another patch (patch three) right sides together with patch two and whip stitch them together as shown. Ensure that the points of patches two and three match perfectly at each end of the seam.

8 Gently bend patch three around—try not to actually crease the paper—and sew it to the center patch along the adjacent edge. Then secure and cut the thread.

9 Sew three more patches around the central patch in the same way as in Steps 7–8, sewing each one to an edge of the previous patch and then to an edge of the central patch. Fit the last patch in place as shown, and sew around the three edges that touch other patches to complete a block.

10 Blocks tessellate together as shown; whip stitch the seams as for individual patches. When the whole patchwork is completed, remove all the basting stitches and the papers.

Crazy patchwork

I adore this style of patchwork as I love the fact that every scrap of lovely fabric in my stash can be put to good use in a crazy patchwork project. Working in a single main color palette can tone the craziness down if you prefer. And machine stitchers will be happy as every element of this sample is done using the sewing machine.

Check out...
Pressing, page 30
Hand embroidery stitches,
   page 83

Best used for...
Lightweight and mediumweight
   fabrics

1.

2.

3.

4.

5.

6.

1 Cut out a starting shape. The edges must be straight, but other than that the patch can be whatever shape you like.

2 Choose a scrap a bit longer along one edge than the starting patch, and pin the pieces right sides together along the long edge.

3 Set the sewing machine to a medium straight stitch and sew the pieces together taking a ¼" (6mm) seam allowance.

4 Open the joined pieces out flat and press the seam, pressing the seam allowances open or to one side, as you prefer. (There seems to be ongoing argument between patchworkers as to which is better; my habit is to press machine-sewn seams open and hand-sewn seams to one side.)

5 Trim off the edges of the second patch so that they align with the adjacent edges of the starting patch. Lay a ruler along the edges and either trim with a rotary cutter, or draw lines and cut along them with scissors.

6 Lay a third piece of fabric right side down across one edge of the two joined patches. Pin then sew the seam, as before.

7 Open out the patch and press the seam allowances, as before.

7.

8.

9.

10.

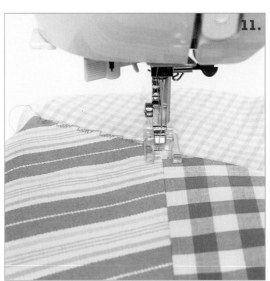

11.

Above: crazy patchwork with machine-embroidered seamlines. If different patterns don't meet neatly at some joins, sewing on a decorative button or motif is a good solution.

8 Continue to add patches in this way, sewing each new piece to straight edges of one or more previous patches, and pressing it flat.

9 Edges will quickly become long, and if you want to add smaller pieces, simply join as many as you wish into a larger patch, and sew that to a straight edge of the original piece.

10 Traditionally, the seams were embellished with hand embroidery, and if you enjoy doing that (as I do) then it is a lovely option. Use stranded or perlé floss and simply work your favorite stitches along the seamlines between patches.

11 However, the embroidery stitches available on modern sewing machines work brilliantly for embellishing crazy patchwork seams, so do experiment with what they have to offer.

Choosing fabrics

You can use fabrics of all types in crazy patchwork, though it can be hard to use both very lightweight and heavyweight fabrics in the same project without the lighter fabric distorting. It's unlikely that you will ever want to—or be able to— launder a crazy patchwork, so you don't need to worry about fiber compatability from that point of view.

Trapunto quilting

The name is from the Italian verb "to embroider", and the technique produces distinctive stitched and raised designs that look good as single motifs in an otherwise flat project, or worked as an overall trapunto design.

Above: the effect of trapunto is quite subtle and elegant.

Check out...
Running stitch, page 33

Best used for...
Lightweight and mediumweight fabrics

1 Draw the design you want to work onto the right side of the backing fabric. Then lay the main fabric right side down and the backing fabric right side up on top of it. Pin the layers together.

2 Baste the layers together around the design.

3 Thread a slim needle with sewing thread. Work very small running stitches around the marked design. Remember that you are working on the back and that the stitches on the front need to be neat; so keep checking that the front looks good. Secure the thread with a few backstitches into the backing fabric only, within the design outline. Remove the basting threads.

4 Using small, sharp scissors, very carefully cut a slit in the backing fabric; do not cut the main fabric or any of the stitches.

5 Use tweezers or the tip of a knitting needle to push some stuffing through the slit. Add just a little stuffing at a time to fill the stitched design area, but do not stuff it hard.

6 Sew the slit closed with lacing stitches. Make each stitch from the inside to the outside, as shown, and make them quite deep so that the cut edges are drawn smoothly together.

1.

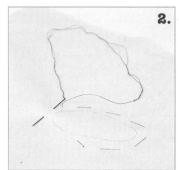

2.

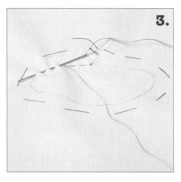

3.

4.

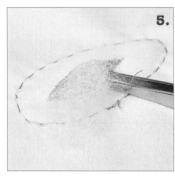

5.

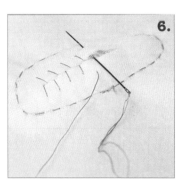

6.

piping, pleating, patchwork...

Tied quilting

If you want to make a quilt, but the idea of actually quilting worries you, then you can tie the layers together. The technique is shown here on a single piece of fabric, but works equally well on patchwork, and is done once the layers of the quilt (top, batting, and backing) have been basted together.

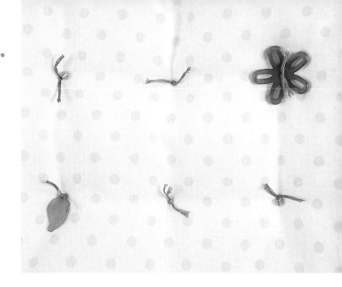

Check out...

Needles, page 21

Best used for...

All fabrics

1 Thread a crewel needle with a length of stranded or perlé embroidery floss. Make a single stitch through all three layers of the quilt, leaving a 2" (5cm) tail of floss free.

2 Make a second single stitch the required distance away, leaving a loop of floss between them. The ties can be spaced as you wish (I have used two spots of this fabric as a guide), but they shouldn't be more than 4" (10cm) apart, and the loop of floss between them must be about 4" (10cm) long.

3 When you have made a row of stitches, leave a 2" (5cm) tail of floss after the last stitch. Cut the loops midway between the stitches, as shown.

4 Tie a single knot, but twist the ends of floss around one another twice, rather than once: this is sometimes called a "surgeon's knot" and won't slip when tightened. Pull this knot as tight as possible, then tie a single knot on top of it to secure it.

5 Trim the ends of the floss to leave short tufts.

6 You can embellish the quilt further by tying on buttons, beads, or charms. Make the surgeon's knot, then thread on the charm, then tie a second knot. Do bear practicality in mind and don't tie sharp things to anything that'll touch the skin, and never tie items to a baby quilt.

1.

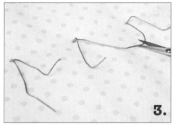

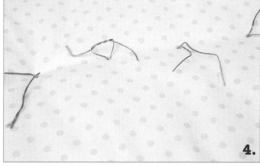

5.

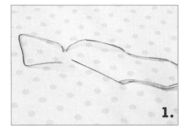

2.

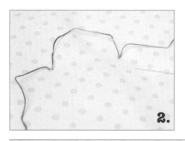

4.

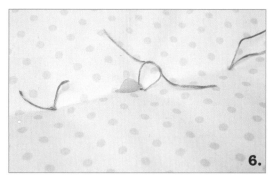

6.

Above: these ties are embellished with beads, a leaf charm, and a flower button.

Things to make

The main point of acquiring new sewing skills—and perfecting those already learned—is to make lovely things for yourself, your family, and friends. The projects here are designed to put into context some of the techniques shown in this book, and hopefully inspire you to make your own pieces using other techniques.

Yo-yo scarf

This lush and textural scarf is deceptively easy to make. I have used richly-colored velvet and silk, but any two fabrics can be used: try chambray and linen for a muted, elegant look, or two bright prints for a hippy-chick feel, or vivid plain colors for a color-blocking vibe.

You will need...

60" x 10" (150 x 25cm) of fabric for the front

60" x 10" (150 x 25cm) of fabric for the back

Small amounts of both fabrics for the yo-yos

Compasses or plates and cups of different sizes

Fusible webbing

Iron

Ironing board

Hand sewing needle

Stranded embroidery floss

Tape measure

Scissors

Pins

Basting thread

Sewing threads to match fabrics

Sewing machine

Walking foot (optional if using velvet)

Check out...

Basting, page 26

Pressing, page 30

Hand utility stitches, page 33

Yo-yos, page 88

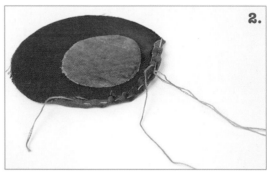

1 Cut circles of the backing fabric for the yo-yos. Iron fusible webbing onto the back of scraps of main fabric and cut smaller circles for the contrast linings. (I used a 5½" (14cm) and a 7" (18cm) plate and a 2½" (6cm) cup as templates.) Iron the smaller circles onto the larger ones, positioning some of them off-center, although at least 1" (2.5cm) from the edge.

2 When you are sewing on several yo-yos in a small area, it's easier to prepare the gathering floss in advance, so finger-press the edge of the large circle and work gathering stitches all around with the floss. Start and end on the wrong side, and do not tie a knot in the floss but leave a 2" (5cm) tail. Do not pull the stitches up tight. Make up as many yo-yos as you require to this stage.

3 Arrange the yo-yos on the scarf front and pin them in place. Make sure that they are at least 1¼" (3cm) from the edges of the scarf front. Using a sewing needle and basting thread, baste the yo-yos in position.

4 Thread the sewing machine with thread to match the yo-yo main fabric and set it to a medium straight stitch. Sew around the edge of each contrast circle. Be careful not to catch the edges of any yo-yos in the stitching. Take out the basting threads.

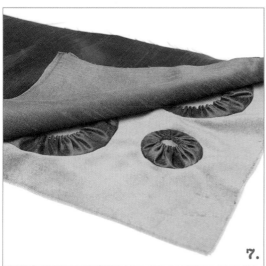

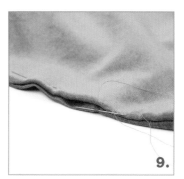

5. One at a time, pull on both ends of the floss to pull up the yo-yos. Do not pull them so tight that the front fabric of the scarf puckers.

6. Knot the ends of the floss firmly, making sure that the knot doesn't show. Thread the ends of floss into a needle and take them through to the back. Secure them on the back of the yo-yo by making a couple of stitches though the scarf-front layer only.

7. Right sides together, lay the scarf back over the scarf front, matching all raw edges. Pin the layers together. If you are using velvet, or another tricky fabric, then you might want to baste the layers.

8. Taking a ⅝" (1.5cm) seam allowance, machine sew around the edges, leaving a 6" (15cm) gap in the middle of one long edge. I rounded off the corners as I sewed, but that is optional. If you are using velvet or another slippery fabric, you might find a walking foot useful, though I didn't find that I needed one here.

9. Trim the seam allowances if necessary. Turn the scarf right side out through the gap. Turn in the seam allowances and ladder stitch the gap closed. Press just the seams all around.

Christmas decoration

These decorations are entirely hand-made, but will come together more quickly than you might imagine. And as they are so small, they lend themselves to being worked on in front of the television, or at odd moments between other tasks. And small children can help with sewing on the sequins, while slightly older ones can work the blanket stitch edgings—beaded or not, as their skills allow. The steps show the heart being made, but the methods are the same for any shape

You will need...

5" x 10" (12 x 24cm) of felt
8" (20cm) of narrow velvet ribbon
Template on page 126
Paper for template
Pins
Scissors
Beading thread to match sequins
  and fabric
Beading needle
Sequins and beads for decoration
Small seed beads for edging
Toy stuffing

Check out...

Hand utility stitches, page 33
Sequins, page 80

VARIATION
The gray decoration is tear-drop
shaped, with pink snowflakes, circular
sequins, and beads.

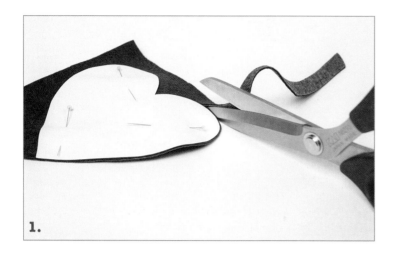

1.

2.

3.

1 Photocopy the template and cut it out. Pin it to the felt and cut out two shapes.

2 Thread the beading needle with thread to match the sequins. Start sewing sequins and beads onto one felt piece in whatever arrangement you wish: I started on one lobe and worked across and down the heart.

3 Fold the ribbon in half and sew it on as shown to form a hanging loop for the heart. Cover the stitches by sewing on a final sequin.

4.

5.

4 Pin the two pieces wrong sides together. Starting at the ribbon loop, work beaded blanket stitch to join the edges all around. To do this, pick up a bead and slide it down to sit next to the last stitch worked, then take the needle through the edges of the felt and loop the working thread under it to make the stitch. Pull the stitch tight and the bead will lie on the edge of the heart. Repeat on every stitch to make the pretty edging.

5 Before completing the stitching, stuff the decoration with toy stuffing, using the blunt end of a knitting needle to push it into all the corners. Then finish the beaded edge stitching.

VARIATION
The blue decoration is oval and has silver snowflake sequins, green circular sequins and seed beads, and tiny black star sequins.

Zip-up bag

I make dozens of these bags; as gifts, as make-up bags, one for my crochet hooks, projects bags, one for the dog's treats on walks...They have many, many uses, and they are great stash busters, and they look good. Ideal all round. The installation of the zipper might seem a bit counter-intuitive at first, but follow the directions carefully and it will make sense.

You will need...

9" x 6¾" (23 x 17cm) of fabric for
the outer

9" x 6¾" (23 x 17cm) of fabric for
the lining

4¾" (12cm) metal zipper

Template on page 126

Paper for template

Scissors

Pins

Basting thread

Sewing threads to match fabrics

Hand sewing needle

Sewing machine

Zipper foot

Iron

Ironing board

Scrap of ribbon

Check out...

Pressing, page 30

Hand utility stitches, page 33

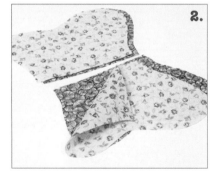

1 Photocopy the template and cut it out. Pin it to the fabrics and cut out two outers and two inners. They need to be mirror images, so either fold the fabrics wrong side together and cut through two layers together, or flip the template to cut the second piece.

2 Pair up the pieces with an outer and a lining right sides together, the lining on top, as shown.

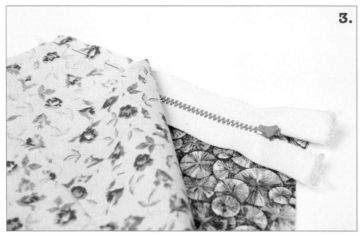

3 Face down, slip the zipper between the straight edge of the fabrics, sliding it right in so that the raw edges of the fabric match the edge of the furthest tape. Pin the fabrics to that zipper tape, thereby completely covering the whole zipper.

4 Set the sewing machine to a medium straight stitch and fit a zipper foot. Stitch along the zipper, about ¼" (6mm) from the teeth.

5 Open the fabrics out so they are both right sides up and the zipper is visible, although face down. Machine-sew along the edge of the lining fabric, understitching it to the zipper tape and the seam allowances: this will stop it catching in the teeth when the zipper is opened. Fold both fabrics wrong sides together so the zipper is visible.

6 Repeat Steps 3–5 to attach the other pieces of fabric to the other side of the zipper. Take your time and do this methodically, and once you have pinned the zipper in place—before you stitch it—open the fabrics right sides out to check that you have pinned correctly: you should have a visible zipper with a right side lining and a right side outer attached to each tape. When you are understitching the lining, it will all look as shown.

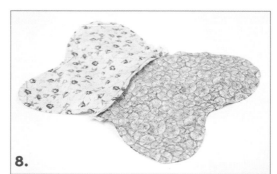

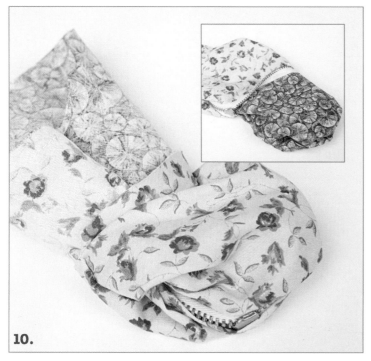

7 Fold the fabrics with the outers right sides together and linings right sides out. Using a sewing needle and thread, whip stitch the ends of the zipper tapes as shown. Leave a small space between the teeth and the whip stitching. Undo the zipper halfway: this is vital.

8 Now fold the fabrics so that the outers are right sides together and the inners are right sides together, as shown. Pin the fabrics together around the edges.

9 Fit a straight stitch foot and, starting in the middle of the bottom edge of the lining and taking a ⅜" (1cm) seam allowance, sew all around the lining and outer, stopping 3" (8cm) before the start of the stitching to leave a gap.

10 Turn the bag right side out through the gap in the lining, then pull the outer right side out through the half open zipper (that's why it was vital to open it before sewing around the bag).

11 Turn in the seam allowances and ladder stitch the gap in the lining closed. Then push the lining into the outer. Push out all the corners and smooth the seams with your fingers, then press them.

12 Tie a piece of ribbon to the zipper pull to finish it off cheerfully.

Crazy patchwork cushion

Working crazy patchwork in a minimal palette will dial down the craziness without losing the patchwork aesthetic. Make full use of gorgeous scraps from your stash, and add trims and decorative stitches to your heart's content.

You will need...

17¼" x 13¼" (43 x 33cm) of backing fabric for the front
2 11" x 13¼" (28 x 33cm) pieces of fabric for the back
Scraps of fabrics for the patchwork
Scrap of trim
Buttons for decoration
Embroidery flosses
Embroidery needle
16" x 12" (40 x 30cm) cushion pad
Tape measure
Fabric marker
Scissors
Pins
Ruler
Basting thread
Sewing threads to match fabrics
Hand sewing needle
Sewing machine
Iron
Ironing board

Check out...

Pressing, page 30
Hand utility stitches, page 33
Hand embroidery stitches, page 83
Crazy patchwork, page 96

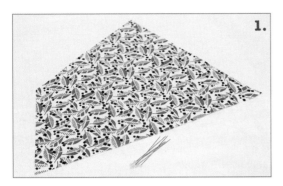

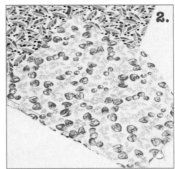

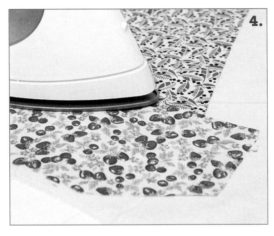

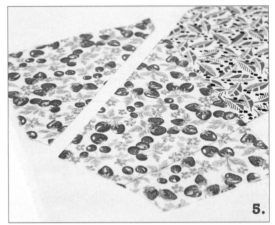

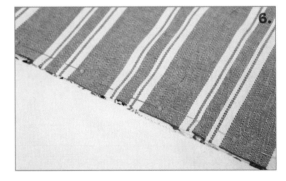

1 As it will not be quilted, this patchwork is made on a backing fabric to give it strength. Start by pinning the central patch to the middle of the front backing fabric (here, cream curtain lining, but any plain, mediumweight fabric will work).

2 Right sides together, pin a second patch to one edge.

3 Set the sewing machine to a medium straight stitch and machine-sew the second patch to the first patch and to the backing fabric.

4 Fold the patch out right side up and press the seam.

5 Use a ruler and fabric marker to draw lines on the second patch to match it up with the edges of the first one. Then carefully cut off the excess with scissors.

6 To add a piece of trim, such as jumbo rick-rack, to the patchwork, you need to sandwich one end between two patches so that the end will be sewn into the seam. So pin the trim to the right side of the relevant patch, then lay that patch face down on the one it will be sewn to. Here, you can see the backs of the pins holding the rick-rack to the patch and the end of the rick-rack peeking out of the seam. Sew the seam, open out the patch and press the seam, as before.

7 Sew the rick-rack to the patch with pick stitch.

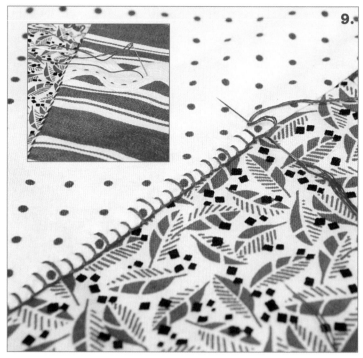

8 Continue adding patches until all the backing fabric is covered with crazy patchwork. Trim the edges of the patches all around to match the edges of the backing fabric and pin the layers together. Fit a zigzag foot and set the sewing machine to a medium zigzag stitch. Zigzag right around the edge of the patchwork, sewing through all layers.

9 Embellish the seams with embroidery stitches, by hand or by machine. For this—quite small—project I hand-embroidered. Here is blanket stitch with the "legs" at different lengths, and running stitches on the rick-rack.

10 Buttons can be sewn on for further embellishment; I used vintage linen ones that went with the color palette and complemented the vintage look of the patchwork.

11 Fit a straight stitch foot and set the sewing machine to a medium straight stitch. Turn under a double ⅜" (1cm) hem on one short edge of each piece of backing fabric.

12 Right sides together, lay one backing piece on the patchwork front, hem towards the middle and matching the raw edges. Then lay the other piece on top in the same way. (For an envelope back with no buttons you want a generous overlap to stop the cushion pad peeking out of the opening.)

13 Taking a ⅝" (1.5cm) seam allowance, machine-sew around the edges of the cushion: I found it easiest to do this on the cushion front as shown here. Turn the cushion cover right side out and insert the pad.

Table runner

Elegant and practical, a runner along the center of your table can be used to stand dishes on, or left there between meals to dress the table. The mitring technique isn't difficult, it just needs careful and accurate pressing, so you could make napkins to match your runner if you like a coordinated look. This runner measures 40" x 12" (100 x 30cm).

You will need...

40" x 12" (100 x 30cm) of fabric for
   the inner section
44½" x 16½" (112 x 42cm) of fabric
   for the backing and border
Tape measure
Measuring gauge
Scissors
Pins
Sewing thread to match fabric
Sewing machine
Iron
Ironing board

Check out...

Pressing, page 30
Turning out and pressing a corner,
   page 32
Topstitched seam, page 43
Machine-embroidered hem, page 58

1 Measure and press under a ¾" (2cm) hem all around the backing piece of fabric, then press under a 1½" (4cm) hem all around.

2 Open the pressed hems out and lay the fabric right side down. At the corner, fold over a triangle of fabric: the point where the second pressed lines cross should be in the middle of the folded-over edge. Press the corner fold flat.

3 Open the corner out, then fold it in half, right sides together, matching the raw edges and the ends of the pressed corner fold. Pin along the pressed corner fold, with the head of the pin facing toward the raw edges of the fabric.

4 Set the sewing machine to a medium straight stitch. Starting at the fold, machine-sew along the pressed corner line as far as the first pressed hem line, reversing at each end to secure the stitching.

5 Trim off the corner of fabric ¼" (6mm) above the line of stitching. At the folded edge, clip off a little more fabric at an angle, as shown.

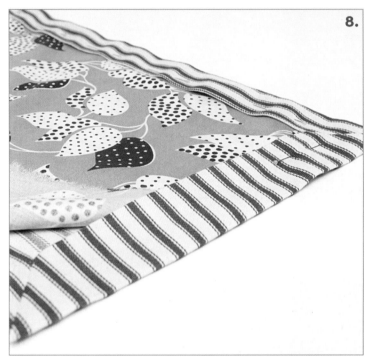

Stitches

I took this opportunity to use one of the decorative stitches that my sewing machine offers—and that so rarely get used. Do test a stitch out on scraps of the project fabric—layered up to match the thickness of the project itself—to get the stitch tension right. However, the runner works just as well if the border is simply topstitched with straight stitch, and indeed, if you are using a patterned fabric for the backing, plain topstitching may well be the better solution.

6 Open the corner out square along the second pressed hemlines. Press the edge trimmed in Step 5 to one side. The clipped angle—which is now at the point—should sit neatly inside the square corner.

7 Turn the corner right side out—use a point turner to help make it neat. Turn under the first pressed hemline and re-press everything so that the corner lies square and flat. Repeat Steps 2–7 on all four corners.

8 Lay the inner fabric flat on the outer, tucking the inner fabric edges under the borders. Spend time making sure that the corners of the inner sit right inside the mitered corners of the backing and that both fabrics are flat and smooth. Pin the inner in place along the border.

9 Fit a zigzag or clearview foot and set the machine to a favorite embroidery stitch. Stitch all around the border ⅝" (1.5cm) in from the edge. Press the runner.

Tablet case

Many of the cases sold to carry and protect your tablet might be practical, but they are all too often unattractive. This easy-to-make case uses quilt batting as a protective layer, and fabrics of your choice for the inner and outer layers, so no excuse not to have a practical and good-looking result.

You will need...

Fabrics for outer and lining
   (see Step 1)
Batting (see Step 1)
Tape measure
Scissors
Pins
Sewing threads to match fabrics
Hand sewing needle
Sewing machine
Iron
Ironing board
Buckle and strap fastening

Check out...

Pressing, page 30
Hand utility stitches, page 33

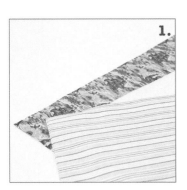

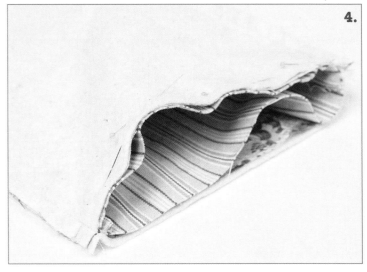

1 Measure the length, width, and depth of your tablet—or laptop (this method also works for a laptop case). Cut two pieces of outer fabric, two pieces of lining fabric and two pieces of batting that each measure the width, plus twice the depth, plus 1½" (4cm), by the width, plus twice the depth, plus 1½" (4cm).

2 Lay out flat a piece of batting, a lining right side up, another lining right side down, and the second piece of batting, as shown.

3 Set the sewing machine to a medium straight stitch and, taking a ⅝" (1.5cm) seam allowance, machine-sew down one long edge of the lining/batting sandwich, turn the

corner and sew along a short distance, then reverse to secure the stitching. Do the same down the other long edge, so that one short edge is completely open and the other has a gap in the middle.

4 Place the two outer pieces of fabric right sides together and sew right around three edges, leaving one short edge open. Turn the outer right side out and press the seams flat.

5 Slip the outer into the open end of the lining/batting sandwich, so that the lining and outer are right sides together, raw edges aligned. Pin the layers together around the open edge.

6 Taking a ⅝" (1.5cm) seam allowance, machine sew around the pinned edge.

7 Turn the whole case right side out through the gap in the lining/batting sandwich. Pull the outer through the gap, as shown, then keep pulling to turn all of the lining right side out.

8 Turn in the seam allowances and ladder stitch the gap in the lining closed.

9 Push the lining down into the outer, making sure the corners are fitting snugly inside one another. Press the top edge of the case.

10 Using a hand-sewing needle and backstitch, sew a buckle and strap fastening to the top of the case to close it. You can use an alternative fastening, but it needs to be something that won't scratch the tablet as you slide it into the case.

Templates

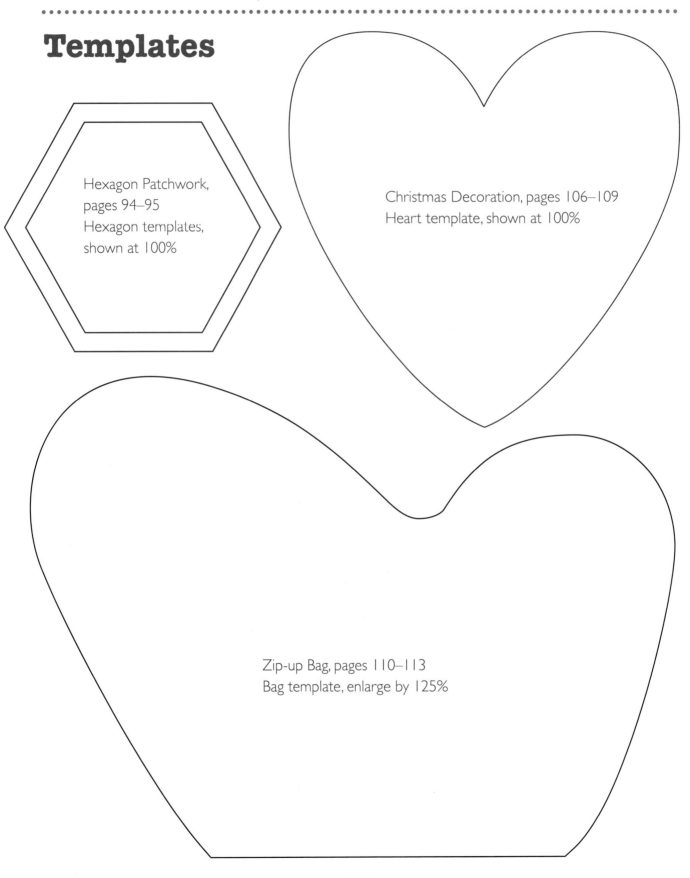

Hexagon Patchwork, pages 94–95
Hexagon templates, shown at 100%

Christmas Decoration, pages 106–109
Heart template, shown at 100%

Zip-up Bag, pages 110–113
Bag template, enlarge by 125%

Resources

LIBERTY OF LONDON
www.Liberty.co.uk
Great Marlborough Street
London W1B 5AH
Tel: 011 44 20 7734 1234
Supplier of Liberty fabrics

REPRODEPOT FABRICS
www. Reprodepot.com
Supplier of vintage fabrics.

SEW, MAMA. SEW!
www.sewmamasew.com
Supplier of cotton fabrics,
magazines, and trims.

JANOME
www.janome.com
The brand of sewing machine
and accessories that I use.

SUPERBUZZY
www.superbuzzy.com
Supplier of imported fabrics,
notions, magazines, and trims.

MOOD FABRICS
www.moodfabrics.com
225 West 37th Street, 3rd Floor
New York, NY 10018
Tel: 212 730 1030
Supplier of garment and
upholstery-weight fabrics,
as well as notions and trims.

FABRITOPIA
www.fabritopia.com
Supplier of a selection of
popular designer fabrics.

THE COTTON PATCH
www.quiltsusa.com
Supplier of a wide selection
of fabrics and sewing machines.

Acknowledgments

I was once again very lucky to have a fabulous team to work with on
this book: Dominic Harris took the great photographs and Louise Leffler
put the pages together beautifully. Molly Small was the lovely model. My
thanks to Paula Breslich for commissioning the book. Lisa at Stealthbunny
(www.stealthbunny.co.uk) lent me the lovely buttons used in the fastenings
chapter. And thanks, as always, to Philip for the food and for putting up
with it all.

Index